DEBT RECOVERY IN TH

DEBT RECOVERY IN THE COUNTY COURT

M. A. BARRY FICM

Croner Publications Ltd
Croner House
London Road
Kingston upon Thames
Surrey KT2 6SR
Telephone: 081–547 3333

Copyright © 1992 Croner Publications Ltd
First published 1992

Published by
Croner Publications Ltd,
Croner House,
London Road,
Kingston upon Thames,
Surrey KT2 6SR

Tel: 081-547 3333

While every care has been taken
in the writing and editing of this book,
readers should be aware that only Acts of Parliament
and Statutory Instruments have the force of law,
and that only the courts can authoritatively
interpret the law.

British Library Cataloguing in Publication Data
A CIP Catalogue Record for this book
is available from the British Library

ISBN 1 85542 118 8

Printed by Redwood Press Ltd
Melksham, Wiltshire

Contents

List of Illustrations

Introduction

In July 1991 significant changes were made to the civil court system. As a result trade debts of *any* value may now be recovered through the county courts. Creditors have the facility to issue their own county court proceedings without using solicitors. In doing so they must bear in mind that the county courts are not "official debt collectors". They are part of the civil justice system.

Thus, just because a creditor sues a debtor, the courts do *not* assume that the debtor is "in the wrong". They assume that there is a dispute between the parties and that the creditor, by issuing proceedings, has asked the courts to resolve that dispute.

The courts have established systems and procedures to do that. They do not "take sides"; they do not *work for* the creditor. They are an independent organisation designed to investigate and settle disputes.

An initial sign of that independence is that the courts regard the creditor as "the plaintiff" and the alleged debtor as "the defendant".

The creditor who decides to use the court system thus has to understand the system and make it work.

The process

The creditor (the plaintiff) issues a default summons. The summons is served, ie delivered, to the debtor (the defendant) with a set of instructions defining the steps that can be taken to deal with it.

If the defendant ignores the summons then, after a fixed number of days have elapsed, the plaintiff is entitled to judgment.

Judgment

However, the courts will not give judgment automatically. The plaintiff must apply for it and it will then be entered. The courts will send a copy of the judgment to the defendant, stating that it has been "adjudged" (decided) that a defined sum of money is payable to the plaintiff. The judgment warns that if payment is *not* made steps may be taken to *enforce* payment — to compel the defendant to pay.

Enforcement

The courts will not, however, take any enforcement action unless and until the plaintiff requests them to do so.

The courts provide a range of enforcement actions which the plaintiff can use and it is for him or her to decide which steps to take.

Thus, the courts provide the system and the plaintiff must make that system work.

Understanding the system — what it can do and what it cannot do — is essential to any creditor who decides to use it.

This book is designed to assist creditors to progress claims for trade debts successfully through the county court system.

It is *not* offered as a legal text book but as a practical working guide for the business or company wishing to "do its own court work" successfully.

Chapter 1

The County Court System

County courts have jurisdiction (power) to deal with claims for trade debts of *any* value. Most major towns have a county court; in the Greater London area there are courts for each borough (eg Wandsworth, Lambeth, etc).

County courts cover England and Wales but not Scotland or Northern Ireland. County court addresses and telephone numbers are set out in Appendix 1.

A creditor may bring a claim in *any* county court, not necessarily in his or her local court, or the debtor's court. The creditor may thus find it more convenient to issue all summonses in the nearest one, but the creditor can choose any court. If, however, the debtor disputes the claim the case will be transferred to the *debtor's* county court for hearing.

Claims of £1000 or less which are disputed will be dealt with by "informal arbitration". This is a hearing before the district judge, in his or her office and is designed to enable disputes concerning "small claims" to be resolved with minimum delay, cost and formality.

County court personnel

County courts vary in size, some employing more staff than others, depending on the volume of work carried by that particular court. Court personnel are as follows:

(a) judge who hears and determines cases in "open court"
(b) district judge who deals with informal arbitration and has power to determine claims up to £5000. A district judge also deals with disposal hearings, pre-trial reviews and the hearing of various interim and enforcement applications
(c) chief clerk who is responsible for the over-all management of the court and has, in addition, some quasi-judicial functions concerning disposals, suspension of warrants, attachments and consent orders
(d) court clerks who are the administrative staff of the court and deal with the paperwork and day to day court functions
(e) bailiffs who are responsible for the enforcement under warrants of execution, the service of summonses and orders and the enforcement of committal orders.

Court forms

All county courts use standard forms and provide them free of charge. Good quality photocopies are acceptable but the court can reject any documents that are illegible or unsatisfactory in any way.

All court forms have a designated number which is printed on each form (for example, a default summons is an N1, a notice of issue of default summons is an N205A) and court staff will frequently refer to forms by number rather than by name.

Court fees

The courts charge fixed fees for the issue of summonses and enforcement actions. Fees are paid, on issue, by the creditor and are added to the amount claimed. Thus the debtor becomes liable for the fee in addition to the debt.

Fees may be paid in cash or by cheque made payable to "H.M. Paymaster General". Those quoted in Appendix 2 are current at the date of publication. They do change from time to time and creditors can always check the current level with their local court.

Costs

If a solicitor issues a summons or other process on behalf of a creditor, he or she can charge a fixed sum — "scale costs" *against the debtor* for the work involved.

A creditor who does not use a solicitor is known as a "creditor in person" and cannot charge the debtor any sum for "costs". But if a creditor incurs travel and other reasonable expenses in attending a hearing and wins the case, the court may order the debtor to pay those expenses, or a reasonable proportion thereof. The decision rests entirely with the court.

"Bulk issue" of process

Creditors who deal with a high volume of court work and who wish to centralise all their work in one court should first contact the chief clerk of that court to ensure that the chosen place is the most appropriate one in terms of staffing and resources.

The county courts have established "bulk issue" procedures, using computer tape, to deal with high volume users. The chief clerk of any county court can put appropriate creditors in touch with the Bulk Issue Office.

Dealing with "foreign" debtors

Creditors may wish to recover from debtors outside England and Wales. For example, a debtor may live or carry on business in Scotland or France or any other country which will have its own laws and court procedures.

Proceedings can be issued in a county court and the creditor can ask for permission to have the summons served "out of the jurisdiction". In effect the creditor is asking the court for leave to serve the summons on someone over whom the English courts have no power or control. Such leave is often given but the debtor may acknowledge the summons and "protest the jurisdiction". That means that he or she disputes the right of the English courts to determine the matter, on the ground that the debtor is a foreigner, not bound by English law and that the debtor's court is the appropriate one to decide the issue.

In those circumstances there is usually a hearing to determine the initial point of which court has the right to determine the dispute. This can cause delay and additional expense. To avoid this, the creditor may well decide to instruct a lawyer in the country concerned. The creditor can do this and the case will then be determined in the courts of that country, in accordance with *its* laws and procedures.

Another option is to stipulate in any contract or in the terms and conditions of sale that: "The proper law of all transactions between the parties is English law and any disputes arising shall be determined by the Courts in England". Then, if a dispute does arise, action can be taken in the county court in England. The parties have agreed, in advance, that this is the position. Thus, the creditor may obtain judgment in the local county court. It is, of course, a judgment of an English court.

If the debtor has assets in England action may be taken to enforce the judgment through the county court. If, however, the debtor has no premises or assets in England the judgment must be enforced in the country concerned, through its courts and in accordance with its procedures.

Brussels Convention 1968

Under the Brussels Convention of 1968, adopted into United Kingdom law in January 1987, all EC Member States, with the exception of Spain and Portugal, now recognise and enforce each other's judgments.

If, therefore, the debtor is in an EC country (other than Spain or Portugal) the creditor can instruct a lawyer in that country to enforce the judgment.

Lugano Convention 1989

As a result of the Lugano Convention of September 1989, between the EC and EFTA, countries in EFTA have the same reciprocal arrangements.

Obviously it is an advantage if the creditor can fight in the local county court and enforce in the foreign country. If that is impractical then the best alternative is to instruct a lawyer in the debtor's country.

Chapter 2

The Decision to Sue

Having exhausted all the usual means of account collection the creditor may decide to resort to legal action.

Before issuing proceedings it is usual to write giving notice to the debtor. There is no rule that requires the creditor to give seven days notice. Nor should the creditor use a summons form, or any other document that looks as though it has some official authority, as a "threat".

A simple letter, giving particulars of the debt and the intended action, is all that is necessary. (Figure 2.1 is an example.) If that letter is ignored it is important to take court action without further delay.

In making the decision to sue the creditor must consider three basic questions:

1. Who is the debtor?
2. Can the creditor *prove* the claim?
3. Does the debtor have the ability to pay?

The effectiveness of the court system depends on these three questions. The "quality" of the debt determines the outcome of the action. A creditor who puts "bad debts" through the court system is simply wasting time and money.

1. Who is the debtor?

This is perhaps a strange question but one that many creditors find difficult to answer. It is significant that in *Credit Management*, August 1991, the Chief Executive of the Registry of County Court Judgments wrote:

> In 1990 some 260,000 commercial Judgments were placed on the Register, but far too many of these were registered against the wrong defendant. It seems that plaintiffs do not give a high priority to making sure that they have the correct name of the debtor before issuing a Summons . . .
>
> Not only are these cases extremely unfair and very damaging, but the injured party would probably have good cause for legal action against the plaintiffs for negligence . . .

The debtor will usually be a public limited company, a private limited company, a partnership or an individual. If the debtor is a limited company it must be sued in the name in which it is registered at Companies House.

A partnership can be sued in the partnership name (eg Bloggs & Co (a firm)). It is far better, however, to sue in the name of the partners (eg John Bloggs and Frederick Jones trading as Bloggs & Co (a firm)).

In this way the creditor is seeking to define clearly responsibility for payment. Having obtained judgment, the creditor may find that Bloggs & Co have "ceased to trade", but he has judgment against the firm *and* against John Bloggs *and* against Frederick Jones. The judgment can be enforced against the individuals.

Trade name

An individual may trade in his or her own name, or may adopt a "trade name". John Bloggs may trade as "Owelots". The creditor can sue "Owelots" (a firm) but, again, Owelots may have closed down.

If the creditor had sued "John Bloggs trading as Owelots" then the closure of the business is not a problem. Judgment has been given against "John Bloggs" and can be enforced against *him* even if he has "ceased to trade" or has started some other business in *another* firm name.

Sue in individual's full name

Whenever possible the creditor should sue an individual in the individual's *full* name. A creditor sues "J. Smith" and obtains judgment. When some enforcement action is taken and it is found that there is John Smith, Jane Smith, Joseph Smith, Jack Smith and Jeremy Smith, the court will ask "Which J. Smith do you want?". If the creditor does not know, the court can do little more to help.

Another common "identity" problem arises when a sole trader or partnership adds the words "& Co" or "and Company" to its name. John Smith trades as "John Smith and Company". The *debtor* is "John Smith trading as John Smith & Company".

The creditor, however, may assume that the debtor is "John Smith & Co Limited" and therefore sues in that name. There is no such limited company and so judgment may be entered against an organisation that does not exist: the judgment cannot be enforced.

There may even *be* a John Smith and Company Limited which does not owe the creditor, or anyone else, a penny! Its credit prospects may be damaged because the judgment is registered against it. Such a company may have a right of action against the negligent creditor.

Suing an establishment

It is pointless to sue a building, yet many creditors try to do it! They sue "The Red Lion" or "Fred's Plaice" (the Red Lion is a public house; Fred's Plaice is a fish shop). Those "buildings" are not the debtor. In the case of the Red Lion, it may be the landlord of the Red Lion, in which case the summons needs to name him or her; it may be the brewery, in which case it must be named.

Summary

The correct identity of the debtor must be clearly established and only the creditor can do that.

2. Can the creditor prove the claim?

The courts do not make any assumptions. The creditor, by issuing a summons, alleges that the named "defendant" owes money. If that claim is disputed the onus is on the creditor whose case it is to prove the claim.

Many creditors try to "prove a negative", that is their letters to the debtor say, for example: "As you have not raised any query or complaint we assume you admit liability". They then sue and the debtor denies liability. Very often the creditor takes the view that the debtor has not denied liability before legal action and it is too late to do so now. The courts do not have to accept that view.

The role of the courts is to determine the facts and to make a decision.

Good documentation

First, they require the creditor to prove the claim. The secret of success lies in good documentation: clearly documented orders, well defined terms, positive proof of delivery, etc.

Good documentation often wins cases; poor documentation or no documentation at all loses them.

3. Does the debtor have the ability to pay?

Getting judgment can be easy but turning it into money is often more difficult. There are steps that can be taken against a debtor who will not pay that may change his or her mind. But if the debtor is unable to pay then nothing will change the situation. No system can extract money from people who have none.

The message is very clear: if creditors extend credit to those who do not have the ability to pay then they will not get paid.

These three basic questions highlight the importance of good credit control. A creditor with effective credit control systems will meet with success in court actions, but one who regards the courts as a back stop for poor credit control will fail.

A "clean" and proveable debt is an essential element of success in court. The issue of a summons is not designed to frighten the debtor so that he or she abandons his or her query or complaint. Indeed, with the summons the debtor is given a set of instructions and forms to enable queries and disputes to be recorded.

Defended claim

The creditor then faces a "defended" claim. The courts must now fix a date for a hearing and the creditor must prove the claim and be able to deal with the query or complaint raised by the debtor.

Good credit control procedures will have identified and solved the genuine queries and should show that all other problems are spurious.

Summary

The key elements for successful court action are:

(a) correct customer identity
(b) good documentation
(c) creditor's ability to prove the claim
(d) a "clean" debt
(e) a debtor with the ability to pay.

Dear Sir(s),

Overdue Account: £750.

The above sum remains unpaid despite previous reminders.

We now give you formal notice that unless we receive payment in full by _____ we will, immediately thereafter, commence Court proceedings against you.

This will involve additional claims for Court fees and interest which will significantly increase the sum you may have to pay.

It is thus in your own interest to ensure that payment in full is made within the time limited by this letter.

Yours faithfully,

Figure 2.1 Standard form of letter before action

Chapter 3

Starting an Action in the County Court

Actions to recover a trade debt begin with the issue of a default summons. It is called a "default" summons because it sets out the creditor's claim, informs the debtor of the steps to be taken to deal with it and warns that if the recipient does not respond the creditor may obtain judgment "in default".

Form N1

The creditor prepares the form of summons using a standard Form N1 available from the county court (Figure 3.1). The front of the form is completed by the creditor. The reverse side contains instructions to, and information for, the debtor.

The creditor must provide one copy of N1 for the court and one for each defendant. The form must be completed in black ink or type and clear, clean copies must be produced. Photocopies *may* be accepted if they are clear and accurate. Both sides of the form must be copied. The court has the right to reject poor or illegible copies.

Completing the form of summons

The name of the county court which the creditor is using should be entered in the space provided.

When issuing the summons, the court will allocate a case number to the action. This must then be quoted on all subsequent forms, letters and documents submitted to the court.

The remaining parts of the form are completed as follows.

Plaintiff's full name and address

Here the name and address of the creditor is inserted. If the creditor is a limited company the full name of the company, as registered at Companies House, must be used. The address must be the registered office of the company and this is indicated by putting the letters "r.o." or the words "registered office" *before* the address.

If the creditor is an individual, then the full names must be used (eg John Michael Smith not J.M. Smith or John M. Smith). If the individual has a trading address, that is the address to give. Otherwise the individual's home address is inserted.

A partnership must sue in the names of the partners. Thus, Smith & Co must sue as "John Albert Smith and Mary Elizabeth Smith trading as Smith & Co (a firm)".

Creditors who have a "trade name", for example "Super Supply", must sue in the name of the proprietor or partners (eg "John Brown trading as Super Supply" or "John Brown and Kevin Jones trading as Super Supply").

Address for service and payments

Here the creditor should insert the name and address that the court and the debtor should deal with. A limited company gives its registered office as its address in the first section. The company may want payment and all court papers to go to its accounts department or one of its trading addresses. The address for service and payment is the one that the court will deal with and the one it will direct the debtor to deal with.

Defendant's name and address

The correct and full name of the debtor must be given (correctly identifying the defendant is essential: see Chapter 2).

If the debtor is a limited company, the address given may be either the registered office or the trading address. The creditor should identify which it is by putting the words "registered office" or "trading address" *before* the address.

Individuals can be served at their trading address or their home address.

Brief description of the type of claim

The creditor should insert a few words specifying the nature of the claim (eg "Price of goods sold and delivered", "Cost of work done and materials supplied", "Sum due on a dishonoured cheque"). The amount claimed should not be entered in this section, but in the particulars of the plaintiff's claim.

Particulars of the plaintiff's claim

The creditor should use this section to define the value of the claim and how it arises.

In formulating the claim the creditor is entitled to include an element for interest on the debt. The right to interest can arise in one of two ways. The contract, or the creditor's "terms and conditions" may stipulate interest or the creditor can rely on a right to statutory interest.

Interest clause

The creditor is entitled to stipulate interest by incorporating a clause in the contract or terms and conditions, eg:

> We reserve the right to charge interest on accounts which become overdue
> for payment at the rate of . . .

The amount of interest must be defined and many creditors now specify three per cent above the prevailing base lending rate at a named bank.

A creditor who has no such clause in the contract or terms and conditions is still entitled to charge interest but, because the creditor has no right to *contractual* interest the claim is for statutory interest.

Interest runs from the date on which the debt was due to be paid. In cases where the amount claimed is £5000 or less interest stops to run when judgment is entered. When the claim is over £5000 the creditor can claim ongoing interest.

A creditor wishing to claim interest must incorporate this into the initial claim; in other words, must ask for it (the court will not give it automatically).

The creditor must calculate the interest from the date on which the debt was due for payment up to the date of completion of the summons form. For example, claiming statutory interest, the calculation is:

Debt × 15% = A (the annual interest).
A ÷ 365 = D (the daily rate of interest).
Assume, for ease of calculation, that the daily rate is 75p. If, at the date of preparation of the summons the debt is 68 days overdue then the interest to *add* to the claim is 68 × 75p = £51.

The creditor will thus claim the debt plus £51 for interest and will include a claim for ongoing interest at the daily rate of 75p.

To justify the claim for statutory interest the creditor claims it "pursuant to Section 69 of the County Courts Act 1984". This wording is not necessary when the creditor claims "contractual interest".

There is no specified wording for a claim. Figures 3.2 and 3.3 show sample wording that will be acceptable. The suggested wording can be adapted to meet the circumstances.

Dishonoured cheque

There will be cases where a debtor has paid an account by cheque and it has been dishonoured. That means the cheque is returned "refer to drawer". A "stopped" cheque is not dishonoured.

When a cheque is dishonoured the creditor should:

(a) give notice of dishonour
(b) sue *on the cheque*, not for the goods sold or services rendered.

A notice of dishonour is simply written notice addressed to the debtor and giving full details of the cheque, its date, the bank it was drawn on and the fact that it has been dishonoured. A suitable form of wording is shown in Figure 3.4.

If the creditor then sues, the claim is based on the dishonoured cheque, not on the work done or services rendered.

There is, on the face of it, no defence to a dishonoured cheque.

The creditor should not return the cheque to the debtor, but should retain it to be produced, if necessary, as evidence.

A form of claim based on a dishonoured cheque is shown in Figure 3.5. Note that the creditor may claim statutory interest from the date of the cheque. As can be seen, when interest is claimed the creditor does not need to show the calculations on the summons but should simply provide the total figure and the daily rate.

Whenever possible the claim should be set out in the space provided. If there is not sufficient space, then the creditor should type the wording of the claim on plain white A4 paper and staple it to the form of summons. The creditor then signs the claim, striking out the words "plaintiff's solicitor" and inserting the words "for and on behalf of the plaintiff".

The signatory does not have to be a director of the creditor company or a partner in the creditor firm. Anyone authorised to sign by the creditor may do so. The person who signs the claim does not have to attend any hearing. If a hearing is necessary, those who know the facts of the case will attend, as "witnesses".

Completing the figures

In the space provided the creditor inserts the amount claimed. That is the total shown on the summons — the debt plus interest calculated to the date of completion of the form.

The court fee payable on the issue of the summons, calculated as shown in Appendix 2, is inserted in the space provided.

As stated earlier, a creditor "in person", that is a creditor not using a solicitor, cannot claim "solicitor's costs", and should just insert a dash against the item. The total claim is then the debt plus calculated interest plus the court fee.

A completed form of summons is shown in Figure 3.6.

The summons is now ready for issue. The creditor must pay the court fee on presenting the summons for issue. Payment may be made by cheque drawn in favour of "H.M. Paymaster General".

Checklist for issuing a summons

(a) Complete form of summons, one for the court and one for each defendant.

(b) Keep a copy on file for reference.

(c) Take or post forms to the chosen county court with a cheque for the court fee and a stamped return envelope.

Note that if the creditor is issuing several summonses at once he or she may draw one cheque for the total fees payable.

The court will now issue and serve the summons. The creditor is now "the plaintiff" and the debtor is "the defendant". (That is how the parties will be referred to in the case from now on and they will accordingly be referred to in those terms in subsequent chapters of this book.)

County Court Summons

Case Number | Always quote this

In the

County Court

The court office is open from 10 am to 4 pm Monday to Friday

(1)
Plaintiff's
full name
address.

(2)
Address for
service (and)
payment.
If not as above
Ref/Tel no.

Telephone:

(3)
Defendant's
name
address.

Seal

This summons is only valid if sealed by the court.
If it is not sealed it should be sent to the court.

What the plaintiff claims from you

Brief
description
of type of
claim

Particulars of the Plaintiff's claim against you

Amount claimed

Court fee

Solicitor's costs

Total amount

Summons issued on

What to do about this summons

You can

- dispute the claim
- make a claim against the Plaintiff
- admit the claim in full and offer to pay
- pay the total amount shown above
- admit only part of the claim

For information on what to do or if you
need further advice, please turn over.

Signed
Plaintiff('s solicitor)
(or see enclosed particulars of claim)

Keep this summons, you may need to refer to it.

N1   Default summons (fixed amount) {Order 3, rule 3(2)(b)}

Figure 3.1 Form N1

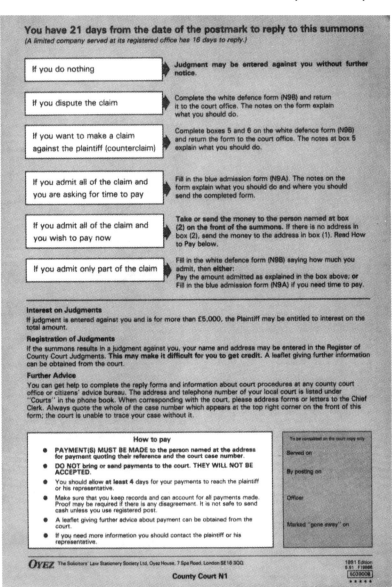

You have 21 days from the date of the postmark to reply to this summons
(A limited company served at its registered office has 16 days to reply.)

If you do nothing	Judgment may be entered against you without further notice.
If you dispute the claim	Complete the white defence form (N9B) and return it to the court office. The notes on the form explain what you should do.
If you want to make a claim against the plaintiff (counterclaim)	Complete boxes 5 and 6 on the white defence form (N9B) and return the form to the court office. The notes at box 5 explain what you should do.
If you admit all of the claim and you are asking for time to pay	Fill in the blue admission form (N9A). The notes on the form explain what you should do and where you should send the completed form.
If you admit all of the claim and you wish to pay now	Take or send the money to the person named at box (2) on the front of the summons. If there is no address in box (2), send the money to the address in box (1). Read How to Pay below.
If you admit only part of the claim	Fill in the white defence form (N9B) saying how much you admit, then either: Pay the amount admitted as explained in the box above; or Fill in the blue admission form (N9A) if you need time to pay.

Interest on Judgments
If judgment is entered against you and is for more than £5,000, the Plaintiff may be entitled to interest on the total amount.

Registration of Judgments
If the summons results in a judgment against you, your name and address may be entered in the Register of County Court Judgments. This may make it difficult for you to get credit. A leaflet giving further information can be obtained from the court.

Further Advice
You can get help to complete the reply forms and information about court procedures at any county court office or citizens' advice bureau. The address and telephone number of your local court is listed under "Courts" in the phone book. When corresponding with the court, please address forms or letters to the Chief Clerk. Always quote the whole of the case number which appears at the top right corner on the front of this form; the court is unable to trace your case without it.

How to pay	To be completed on the court copy only
• PAYMENT(S) MUST BE MADE to the person named at the address for payment quoting their reference and the court case number.	Served on
• DO NOT bring or send payments to the court. THEY WILL NOT BE ACCEPTED.	By posting on
• You should allow at least 4 days for your payments to reach the plaintiff or his representative.	
• Make sure that you keep records and can account for all payments made. Proof may be required if there is any disagreement. It is not safe to send cash unless you use registered post.	Officer
• A leaflet giving further advice about payment can be obtained from the court.	Marked "gone away" on
• If you need more information you should contact the plaintiff or his representative.	

OYEZ The Solicitors' Law Stationery Society Ltd, Oyez House, 7 Spa Road, London SE16 3QQ

1991 Edition
8.91 F19666
5039008

County Court N1

Figure 3.1 (reverse)

The Plaintiffs' claim is £————— the price of goods sold and delivered together with Statutory Interest at 15% per annum pursuant to Section 69 of the County Courts Act 1984.

<u>19</u>   Particulars

Invoice	To goods sold and	
Dates	delivered as per	
	invoices on and	
	between these dates	£(debt)
	Interest thereon	(interest to date)
	Total:	£

The plaintiffs further claim Statutory Interest at the daily rate of (daily rate) until Judgment or (sooner) payment.

Note: the word "sooner" in brackets is <u>omitted</u> when the claim exceeds £5000 because in such cases interest can continue <u>after</u> judgment.

Figure 3.2 Claim for the price of goods sold including a claim for statutory interest

The Plaintiffs' claim is £_____ the cost of work done and materials provided together with interest pursuant to contract.

19	Particulars	

Date of contract	To cost of work done and materials provided pursuant to contract of this date	£(debt)
	Interest thereon	(interest to date)
	Total:	£

The plaintiffs further claim interest pursuant to contract at the daily rate of (daily rate) until Judgment or (sooner) payment.

Note: the word "sooner" in brackets is <u>omitted</u> when the claim exceeds £5000 because in such cases interest can continue <u>after</u> judgment.

Figure 3.3 Claim for the cost of work done and materials provided including a claim for contractual interest

To: A Debtor
       Address   Date of letter

Dear Sir,

Notice of Dishonour

We give you formal notice that your cheque dated _____ and drawn on _____ Bank Limited _____ Branch in our favour in the sum of £_____ has been <u>Dishonoured</u> on presentation.

We require payment of the full amount by cash or Bankers Draft within (three) days.

Yours faithfully,

Figure 3.4 Letter giving notice of dishonour

The Plaintiffs' claim is £_____ the amount due on a cheque drawn by the Defendant in favour of the Plaintiffs and dishonoured on presentation together with Statutory Interest at 15% per annum pursuant to Section 69 of the County Courts Act 1984.

Notice of Dishonour has been given.

Particulars

Date of cheque	To sum due on a cheque drawn on this date on _____ Bank Limited by the Defendant in favour of the Plaintiff and dishonoured on presentation	£	amount of cheque
	Interest thereon	£	amount of interest to date
Total:		£	-

The plaintiffs further claim Statutory Interest at the daily rate of (daily rate) until Judgment or (sooner) payment.

Note: the word "sooner" in brackets is omitted when the claim exceeds £5000 because in such cases interest can continue after judgment.

Figure 3.5 Claim based on a dishonoured cheque including a claim for statutory interest

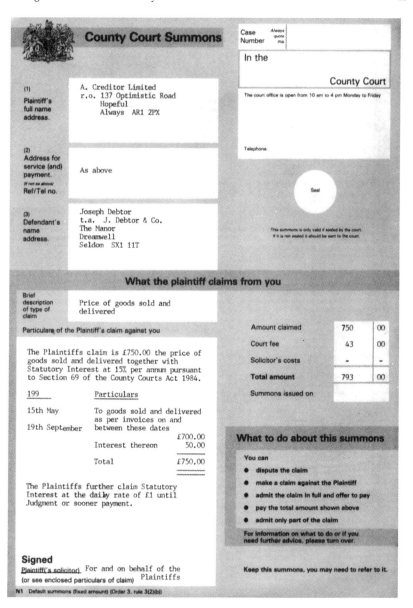

Figure 3.6 Completed form of summons

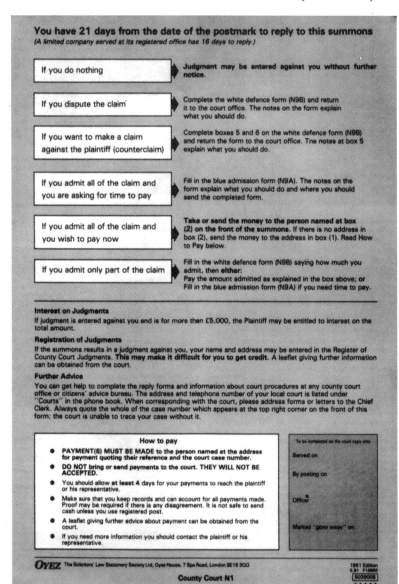

You have 21 days from the date of the postmark to reply to this summons
(A limited company served at its registered office has 16 days to reply.)

If you do nothing	Judgment may be entered against you without further notice.
If you dispute the claim	Complete the white defence form (N9B) and return it to the court office. The notes on the form explain what you should do.
If you want to make a claim against the plaintiff (counterclaim)	Complete boxes 5 and 6 on the white defence form (N9B) and return the form to the court office. The notes at box 5 explain what you should do.
If you admit all of the claim and you are asking for time to pay	Fill in the blue admission form (N9A). The notes on the form explain what you should do and where you should send the completed form.
If you admit all of the claim and you wish to pay now	Take or send the money to the person named at box (2) on the front of the summons. If there is no address in box (2), send the money to the address in box (1). Read How to Pay below.
If you admit only part of the claim	Fill in the white defence form (N9B) saying how much you admit, then either: Pay the amount admitted as explained in the box above; or Fill in the blue admission form (N9A) if you need time to pay.

Interest on Judgments
If judgment is entered against you and is for more than £5,000, the Plaintiff may be entitled to interest on the total amount.

Registration of Judgments
If the summons results in a judgment against you, your name and address may be entered in the Register of County Court Judgments. **This may make it difficult for you to get credit.** A leaflet giving further information can be obtained from the court.

Further Advice
You can get help to complete the reply forms and information about court procedures at any county court office or citizens' advice bureau. The address and telephone number of your local court is listed under "Courts" in the phone book. When corresponding with the court, please address forms or letters to the Chief Clerk. Always quote the whole of the case number which appears at the top right corner on the front of this form; the court is unable to trace your case without it.

How to pay	To be completed on the court copy only
• **PAYMENT(S) MUST BE MADE** to the person named at the address for payment quoting their reference and the court case number.	Served on
• **DO NOT bring or send payments to the court. THEY WILL NOT BE ACCEPTED.**	By posting on
• You should allow at least 4 days for your payments to reach the plaintiff or his representative.	
• Make sure that you keep records and can account for all payments made. Proof may be required if there is any disagreement. It is not safe to send cash unless you use registered post.	Officer
• A leaflet giving further advice about payment can be obtained from the court.	Marked "gone away" on
• If you need more information you should contact the plaintiff or his representative.	

OYEZ The Solicitors' Law Stationery Society Ltd, Oyez House, 7 Spa Road, London SE16 3QQ

County Court N1

1991 Edition
5.91 F16585

S039008

Figure 3.6 (reverse)

Chapter 4

Service of the Summons — the Debtor's Options

The court will "issue", that is "authenticate", the summons. A court clerk will put the court seal on the summons, allocate a case number and date the document. That date is the *issue* date.

The summons will then be "served on", that is delivered to, the defendant. This will be done by posting it to the address given in the summons.

Once the summons is issued, the court will send the plaintiff a Form N205A (Figure 4.1). This confirms the issue of the summons, gives the case number and may indicate the date of service. If it does not give that date, the court will send a further form, N222 (Figure 4.2), confirming the date of service.

Form N205A incorporates a tear off section which the plaintiff can use to apply for judgment in due course. This form gives the plaintiff two important dates and it sets out the defendant's options (things the debtor can do on receiving the summons).

Issue date

This date is the one on which the court entered the claim. From the issue date the defendant is responsible for the debt, the court fee and the interest.

It is the date of issue *not* the date of service that imposes this obligation on the defendant. Thus, if the defendant pays the debt after the issue date, the plaintiff is entitled to the court fee and interest. If the defendant pays the debt and ignores the summons then, when the defendant's time for dealing with the summons is past, the plaintiff can apply for judgment. See "judgment in default", page 35.

Service date

The date of service defined by the court is the date on which it determines the summons will come to the defendant's knowledge.

The defendant has 14 days from that date in which to exercise one of the options open. If he or she ignores the summons then, once the 14 days have expired, the plaintiff is entitled to apply for judgment in default.

Serving the summons is thus essential if progress is to be made. No further action can be taken until this happens.

"Gone away"

The court will post the summons to the defendant in a buff envelope — OHMS. If the defendant is not at the address given the envelope will be returned to the court marked "gone away".

It is possible that the defendant could still be at the given address but, as a matter of practice, may mark all letters which are OHMS "gone away".

If the summons is returned to the court on that basis, it will send the plaintiff notice that the summons has not been served (Form N216, Figure 4.2).

"Personal service"

If the plaintiff has reason to believe that the defendant is still at the given address, then he or she can pay a fee of £5 and ask the court to attempt "personal service" of the summons.

There is no standard form for this request; a letter will suffice which simply refers to the notice of non-service and continues: "We enclose our cheque for £5. Please ask the bailiff to attempt personal service".

On receipt of that letter the court clerk will add £5 to the court fees on the summons (the defendant is liable for the service fee) and pass the summons to one of the court bailiffs who will then go to the given address and attempt to deliver it personally to the defendant.

New address for defendant

It may transpire that the defendant has in fact left this address. The debt may be of sufficient value to justify having enquiries made to trace the defendant. Those enquiries are carried out at the plaintiff's expense. He or she can instruct an enquiry agent or "private detective" to attempt to trace the defendant. If the enquiries are successful and the defendant is traced at an address different to that shown on the summons, the plaintiff will now want the summons served at the new address.

The plaintiff should make a further copy of the summons in identical terms to the original — showing the *old* address of the defendant. Then, he or she should strike out the old address in *red* and insert the new one in *red*. The word "amended" is then written, in *red* under the words "County Court Summons" on the form.

The amended form is then sent or taken to the court. No further fee is payable, but the court will now amend the address on the summons and post it to the defendant at the new address.

The plaintiff may, if service through the court fails, ask for the summons and then attempt service or instruct enquiry agents to "trace and serve". The fee charged by the enquiry agent is not recoverable from the defendant.

Summons is served

Once the summons is served, the defendant has 14 days to deal with it. The summons sets out the claim and, with it, the defendant is given a set of forms telling him or her what to do and enabling the various available options to be exercised.

The options available to the defendant are:

(a) to pay
(b) to ignore the summons
(c) to admit the claim and make an offer to pay

(d) to admit part of the claim and dispute the balance
(e) to dispute all of the claim
(f) to make a claim against the plaintiffs — a counterclaim.

Thus, once the summons is served, the plaintiff must wait 14 days to see which option the defendant decides upon. The defendant's reaction to the summons determines the next step to be taken by the plaintiff.

It is important to understand that the defendant "replies" to the summons by paying the debt or by completing one of the forms served with the summons and returning it to the court or, if appropriate, to the plaintiff.

If the debtor makes payment of the debt in full *after* the issue of the summons then the plaintiff is entitled to apply for judgment for the court fee and interest unless the defendant completes and returns the form provided enabling liability to be disputed.

If the defendant makes a payment on account, but does not complete and return the appropriate form to deal with the balance then, when the 14 day time limit has expired, the plaintiff is entitled to apply for judgment for the balance of the debt plus the court fee and interest up to the date of judgment.

The effect of the various options available to the defendant will now be considered in detail and, in the remainder of this chapter, we will consider the "easy" ones:

(a) the defendant pays or
(b) admits the debt and offers to pay.

The defendant pays

The summons directs the defendant to pay the plaintiffs, not the court. The court will not accept payment under a summons. If the defendant goes to the court with cash it will not be accepted and if the defendant sends or delivers a cheque, the court will send or hand it back to the defendant. The defendant is required to make payment to the plaintiff.

If payment is made in full, or if the defendant makes a part payment, it is not necessary to advise the court.

Receipt

If payment is made in full, the defendant, in making that payment, may ask for a receipt. If payment is by cheque the plaintiff should make sure that the cheque has cleared and can then write to the defendant confirming that the full amount due on the summons has been paid.

Notification of payment

The plaintiff is not required to notify the court of payment. So far as the plaintiff is concerned the action is concluded and he or she will take no further action.

No reply to summons

If the defendant simply pays part of the debt but ignores the summons then, when the 14 day time limit has expired, the plaintiff can apply for judgment for the balance, plus the court fee and the interest up to the date of judgment.

The plaintiff completes the tear off section of Form N205A (Figure 4.1) by ticking Box A "The Defendant has not replied to my Summons". The plaintiff also completes Section C of that form. At that stage the plaintiff has a choice concerning payment of the debt. Simply by ticking the appropriate box the plaintiff can request that judgment be entered for payment:

(a) forthwith (immediately) or
(b) by instalments, in which case the plaintiff stipulates the instalments or
(c) on a fixed date (eg "In full by [a date 7 days after judgment]").

The plaintiff then completes the figure work in Section C: he or she sets out the debt as shown on the summons (which includes the interest on the summons), the court fee paid and the interest that has accrued since the date of the summons.

This section states: "Interest since date of summons (if any)". ("If any" simply refers to whether the plaintiff has claimed interest on the summons or not.) The plaintiff inserts the claim for additional interest based on the number of days that have gone by since the issue of the summons and the application for judgment. There is no need to show any detailed calculations in this section, eg "19 days at 15% — £12".

Section C allows the plaintiff to give credit for any sum paid, after issue, by the defendant and to take judgment for the balance.

For example, a plaintiff sues for a total of £750 for debt and interest. To issue that summons the plaintiff pays a court fee of £43. No solicitors are involved but, after the issue of the summons, the defendant sends the plaintiff £500 but does not otherwise deal with the summons.

Figure 4.3 shows how Form N205A would be completed to apply for judgment for the balance, including the court fee and interest up to the date of the application for judgment.

The same form can be used to take judgment for the court fee and interest in cases where, after the issue of the summons, the defendant pays the debt, but not the court fee or the interest.

The plaintiff lodges the request for judgment with the court. The court clerk will prepare a form of "judgment in default" — Figure 4.4 — and send a copy to the defendant and a copy to the plaintiff.

The plaintiff has "won". It has been "adjudged" (decided) that the defendant must pay the amount shown on the judgment in accordance with its terms. If payment is not made as directed, the plaintiff may take steps to enforce the judgment, that is to compel the defendant to pay.

The defendant admits the debt in full and makes an offer to pay

With the summons the defendant is provided with a set of forms. A blue form, Form N9A (Figure 4.5), enables the debtor to admit the debt and put forward proposals for payment. The offer can be to pay by instalments or to pay the full amount on a fixed date.

A defendant wishing to exercise this option is required to complete the Form N9A and send it to the plaintiffs, *not* to the court. It is then for the plaintiff to decide whether he or she will accept the offer or reject it.

Plaintiff wishes to accept the defendant's offer

The plaintiff uses Form N205A (Figure 4.1) to accept the offer. By ticking the box for "I accept the defendant's proposals for payment" and by completing Section C of the form, the plaintiff indicates acceptance. In doing so, the plaintiff can recover the debt, the court fee is paid, plus any additional interest.

Interest

In claiming additional interest it is not necessary for the plaintiff to show any detailed calculations. The form specifies: "Interest since date of summons (if any). Period ____days. Rate ____%".

The "days" figure is simply the number of days that have gone by since the issue of the summons; the "rate" is the percentage charged. Thus, if the plaintiff is claiming statutory interest this section might say: "14 days at 15% — £10.50".

If the defendant has made any payment since the issue of the summons, credit for the sum paid can be given on the form.

An example of a completed request for judgment is shown in Figure 4.6.

Acceptance of offer

Form N205A is signed and taken or posted to the court. The court clerk will complete a form of judgment, acceptance of offer (Figure 4.7). A copy will be sent, by post, to the defendant and a copy will also be sent to the plaintiff.

The plaintiff is not required to send the court a copy of the defendant's admission and offer. By signing the request for judgment, the plaintiff certifies that the information set out on the form is correct.

The form of judgment tells the defendant that if the judgment is not in accordance with his or her offer he or she should write to the court immediately.

The plaintiff now has judgment for the full amount of the debt, plus the court fee and interest, to be paid in accordance with the defendant's offer. The judgment will indicate the date on which the defendant must make the first payment.

The plaintiff does not accept the defendant's offer

Form N205A is also used to reject an offer made by the defendant. The plaintiff completes Section C indicating his or her proposals for payment. It is possible to ask for payment forthwith, or in full on a fixed date, or for higher instalment payments.

On the reverse of this form (Figure 4.2), the plaintiff can set out objections to the defendant's proposals for payment, but must bear in mind that, in coming to a decision as to payment, the court will be concerned *only* with the defendant's ability to pay. Therefore, "At £5 per month the debt will take too long to repay" is not relevant (or helpful) to the court.

The plaintiff may rely on any information given by the defendant on the admission form and also offer any information he or she has about the defendant.

The completed form should be sent to the court, together with the defendant's form of admission and offer (a photocopy is acceptable).

The court clerk will then consider the available information on the forms and will fix a repayment rate. The parties will be notified of the court's decision by an order for payment (Figure 4.8).

Either party may object to the order and then the court will fix a date for a disposal hearing.

The parties attend before the district judge on the date and at the time fixed. The district judge will consider the figures and listen to any points made by the parties, and will then decide the rate of payment to be made.

The defendant admits the debt but makes no offer

In some actions a defendant may admit the debt but fail to make any offer. By ticking the appropriate box on Form N205A and by completing Section C the plaintiff can apply for judgment and stipulate how payment is to be made.

Checklist — judgment "in default" or on "admission"

(a) *Defendant ignores summons.*
Plaintiff completes Form N205A and sends or takes it to the court office. Judgment is entered "by default".

(b) *Defendant offers full amount by instalments. Plaintiff accepts the offer.*
Plaintiff completes Form N205A, inserting instalments as offered, and sends or takes the form to court. Judgment is entered.

(c) *Defendant offers full amount by instalments. Plaintiff rejects the offer.*
The plaintiff completes Form N205A showing proposals for payment and objections to the defendant's offer. This is sent or taken to court with the defendant's form of offer. The court makes a decision or a disposal date is fixed.

(d) *Defendant admits the debt.*
The plaintiff completes Form N205A, setting out how he or she wishes to be paid. This is taken or sent to court. Judgment is entered on that basis.

Notice of Issue of Default Summons - fixed amount

In the		
	LEEDS	
		County Court

The court office at
LEEDS COMBINED COURT CENTRE,
THE COURTHOUSE, 1 OXFORD ROW, LEEDS LS1 3BG,

is open between 10 am & 4 pm Monday to Friday
Tel:

Case Number	*Always quote this*	

Plaintiff *(including ref.)*

Defendants

Issue date	
Date of postal service	
Issue fee	£

To the plaintiff ('s solicitor)

Your summons was issued today. The defendant has 14 days from the date of service to reply to the summons. If the date of postal service is not shown on this form you will be sent a separate notice of service (Form N222).

The defendant may either

- **Pay** you your total claim.
- **Dispute the whole claim.** The court will send you a copy of the defence and tell you what to do next.
- **Admit that all the money is owed.** The defendant will send you form of admission N9A. You may then ask the court to send the defendant an order to pay you the money owed by completing the request for judgment below and returning it to the court.
- **Admit that only part of your claim is owed.** The court will send you a copy of the reply and tell you what to do next.
- **Not reply at all.** You should wait 14 days from the date of service. You may then ask the court to send the defendant an order to pay you the money owed by completing the request for judgment below and returning it to the court.

For further information please turn over

- -

Request for Judgment

- Tick and complete either A or B. Make sure that all the case details are given and that the judgment details at C are completed. Remember to sign and date the form. Your signature certifies that the information you have given is correct.
- If the defendant has given an address on the form of admission to which correspondence should be sent, which is different from the address shown on the summons, you will need to tell the court.

In the	**LEEDS**	
		County Court
Case Number	*Always quote this*	
Plaintiff		
Defendant		
Plaintiff's Ref.		

A ☐ **The defendant has not replied to my summons**
Complete all the judgment details at C. Decide how and when you want the defendant to pay. You can ask for the judgment to be paid by instalments or in one payment.

B ☐ **The defendant admits that all the money is owed**
Tick only **one** box below and return the completed slip to the court.

☐ **I accept the defendant's proposal for payment**
Complete all the judgment details at C. Say how the defendant intends to pay. The court will send the defendant an order to pay. You will also be sent a copy.

☐ **The defendant has not made any proposal for payment**
Complete all the judgment details at C. Say how you want the defendant to pay. You can ask for the judgment to be paid by instalments or in one payment. The court will send the defendant an order to pay. You will also be sent a copy.

☐ **I do NOT accept the defendant's proposal for payment**
Complete all the judgment details at C and say how you want the defendant to pay. Give your reasons for objecting to the defendant's offer of payment in the section overleaf. Return this slip to the court **together with the defendant's admission** N9A (or a copy). The court will fix a rate of payment and send the defendant an order to pay. You will also be sent a copy.

I certify that the information given is correct

Signed .... **Dated** ....

C Judgment details
I would like the judgment to be paid

☐ (forthwith) *only tick this box if you intend to enforce the order right away*
☐ (by instalments of £   per month)
☐ (in full by   )

Amount of claim as stated in summons
(including interest at date of issue) ....

Interest since date of summons (if any) ....
Period .... Rate .... %

Court fees shown on summons ....

Solicitor's costs (if any) on issuing summons ......

                                                    Sub Total

Solicitor's costs (if any) on entering judgment

                                                    Sub Total

Deduct amount (if any) paid since issue ....

                    Amount payable by defendant

N205A Notice of issue (default summons) and request for judgment (Order 3, rule (2)(d)(1), Order 9 rules 3 and 6)   MCR 2649/SP 91 7/91

Figure 4.1 Notice of issue of summons

Further information

- The summons must be served within 4 months of the date of issue (or 6 months if leave to serve out of the jurisdiction is granted under Order 8, rule 2). In exceptional circumstances you may apply for this time to be extended provided that you do so before the summons expires.

- If the defendant does not reply to the summons or if he delivers an admission without an offer of payment you may ask for judgment. If you do not ask for judgment within 12 months of the date of service the action will be struck out. It cannot be reinstated.

- You may be entitled to interest if judgment is entered against the defendant and your claim is for more than £5000.

- You should keep a record of any payments you receive from the defendant. If there is a hearing or you wish to take steps to enforce the judgment, you will need to satisfy the court about the balance outstanding. You should give the defendant a receipt and payment in cash should always be acknowledged. You should tell the defendant how much he owes if he asks.

- **You must inform the court IMMEDIATELY if you receive any payment before a hearing date or after you have sent a request for enforcement to the court.**

Objections to the defendant's proposal for payment

Case Number

N205A

Figure 4.1 (reverse)

In the LEEDS County Court

Between ....Plaintiff

And ....Defendant

Case No.

Local No.

To the Plaintiff('s Solicitor)

TAKE NOTICE that the:–   Summons ☐

Application ☐

Order ☐

In this action has not been served for the reason ticked below:–

1.   The envelope addressed to the defendant has been returned by the GPO marked:–

NOTE. If you think that the defendant is still at the addresses, you may request bailiff service there on payment of the appropriate fee.

    "Not known at the address given" (see note) ☐

    "Gone away" (see note) ☐

    "No such address" ☐

    "Insufficient address" ☐

2.   The bailiff is unable to trace the address given within the district of this court. ☐

3.   The defendant is not known at the address given. ☐

4.   The defendant is stated to have left the address given. The defendant's new address (if known) is:– ☐

....

....

5.   Premises empty (and boarded up) ☐

6.   Other reason (specify) .... ☐

....

....

AND the Summons ☐

Application ☐

Order ☐

has been returned to the Home Court and any further correspondence should be sent there. ☐

Dated

N.216 – Notice of non-service (general), Order 7 Rules 6(2) and 10(4).   MCR 2649·SP 91 7·91

Figure 4.2 Notice of non-service

Notice of Issue of Default Summons - fixed amount

To the plaintiff ('s solicitor)

In the		
	LEEDS	
		County Court

The court office at
LEEDS COMBINED COURT CENTRE,
THE COURTHOUSE, 1 OXFORD ROW, LEEDS LS1 3BG,

is open between 10 am & 4 pm Monday to Friday
Tel:

Case Number	*Always quote this*	

Plaintiff *(including ref.)*

Your summons was issued today. The defendant has 14 days from the date of service to reply to the summons. If the date of postal service is not shown on this form you will be sent a separate notice of service (Form N222).

The defendant may either

- **Pay** you your total claim.
- **Dispute the whole claim.** The court will send you a copy of the defence and tell you what to do next.
- **Admit that all the money is owed.** The defendant will send you form of admission N9A. You may then ask the court to send the defendant an order to pay you the money owed by completing the request for judgment below and returning it to the court.
- **Admit that only part of your claim is owed.** The court will send you a copy of the reply and tell you what to do next.
- **Not reply at all.** You should wait 14 days from the date of service. You may then ask the court to send the defendant an order to pay you the money owed by completing the request for judgment below and returning it to the court.

Defendants	
Issue date	
Date of postal service	
Issue fee	£

For further information please turn over

Request for Judgment

- *Tick and complete either A or B. Make sure that all the case details are given and that the judgment details at C are completed. Remember to sign and date the form. Your signature certifies that the information you have given is correct.*
- *If the defendant has given an address on the form of admission to which correspondence should be sent, which is different from the address shown on the summons, you will need to tell the court.*

A [✓] **The defendant has not replied to my summons**
Complete all the judgment details at C. Decide how and when you want the defendant to pay. You can ask for the judgment to be paid by instalments or in one payment.

B [ ] **The defendant admits that all the money is owed**
Tick only **one** box below and return the completed slip to the court.

[ ] **I accept the defendant's proposal for payment**
Complete all the judgment details at C. Say how the defendant intends to pay. The court will send the defendant an order to pay. You will also be sent a copy.

[ ] **The defendant has not made any proposal for payment**
Complete all the judgment details at C. Say how you want the defendant to pay. You can ask for the judgment to be paid by instalments or in one payment. The court will send an order to pay. You will also be sent a copy.

[ ] **I do NOT accept the defendant's proposal for payment**
Complete all the judgment details at C and say how you want the defendant to pay. Give your reasons for objecting to the defendant's offer of payment in the section overleaf. Return this slip to the court **together with the defendant's admission** N9A (or a copy). The court will fix a rate of payment and send the defendant an order to pay. You will also be sent a copy.

I certify that the information given is correct

Signed .... Dated ....

In the	**LEEDS**	
		County Court
Case Number	*Always quote this*	
Plaintiff		
Defendant		
Plaintiff's Ref.		

C Judgment details

I would like the judgment to be paid

[✓] (forthwith) *only tick this box if you intend to enforce the order right away*

[ ] (by instalments of £   per month)

[ ] (in full by   )

Amount of claim as stated in summons (including interest at date of issue)	750	00
Interest since date of summons (if any) .... Period 16 Days 15 ... Rate 15 ... %	12	00
Court fees shown on summons	43	00
Solicitor's costs (if any) on issuing summons		
Sub Total	805	00
Solicitor's costs (if any) on entering judgment		
Sub Total	805	00
Deduct amount (if any) paid since issue		
Amount payable by defendant	805	00

N205A Notice of issue (default summons) and request for judgment (Order 3, rule (2)(d)(1), Order 9 rules 3 and 6)   MCR 2649/SP 91 7/91

Figure 4.3 Application for judgment in default

Judgment for Plaintiff
(in default)

Case No.
Always quote this

In the

County Court

The court office is open from 10 am to 4pm Monday to Friday

Plaintiff

Name and address for payment
(if different from above)

Telephone:

Ref/Tel no.

Defendant

Seal

The Defendant has failed to reply to the summons

It is therefore adjudged that
the Plaintiff recover against the Defendant the sum of

for debt (and interest to date of judgment)

and

for costs

amounting together to the sum of

(And the Defendant having paid the sum of)

It is ordered that the Defendant pay the sum of

to the Plaintiff

* *if no sum is shown in this box, payment is due in full by the date shown*

*(by instalments of

for every calendar month,

the first payment to reach the Plaintiff) by

Dated

Take Notice

To the Defendant

If you replied to the summons and judgment has been entered wrongly against you, you should write to the court office shown on this form giving your reasons why the judgment should be set aside. A hearing will be arranged and you will be told when to come to court. If this judgment is not from your local county court, it will automatically be transferred to that court for hearing.

If you do not pay in accordance with this order your goods may be removed and sold or other enforcement proceedings may be taken against you. If your circumstances change and you cannot pay, ask at the court office about what you can do.

This judgment has been registered in the Register of County Court Judgments. **This may make it difficult for you to get credit.**

When the money is paid in full (including any interest*) you can ask the court to mark the entry in the register as satisfied and for a certificate proving payment. You will have to provide proof and pay a fee. **If you pay in full within one month of judgment the entry will be removed.**

*If judgment is for more than £5,000, the plaintiff may be entitled to interest.

N30 Judgment for plaintiff in default (Order 22, rule 1(1)).

How to Pay

● **PAYMENT(S) MUST BE MADE to the person named at the address for payment quoting their reference and the court case number.**

● **DO NOT bring or send payments to the court. THEY WILL NOT BE ACCEPTED.**

● You should allow <u>at least</u> 4 days for your payment to reach the Plaintiff or his representative.

● Make sure that you keep records and can account for all payments made. Proof may be required if there is any disagreement. It is not safe to send cash unless you use registered post.

● A leaflet giving further advice about payment can be obtained from the court.

● If you need more information you should contact the Plaintiff or his representative.

Figure 4.4 Judgment in default

Admission

In the

County Court

When to fill in this form

- Only fill in this form if you are admitting all or some of the claim and you are asking for time to pay
- If you are disputing the claim or you wish to pay the amount claimed, read the back of the summons

Case Number *Always quote this*

Plaintiff *(including ref.)*

Defendant

How to fill in this form

- Tick the correct boxes and give as much information as you can. Then sign and date the form.
- Make your offer of payment in box 11 on the back of this form. If you make no offer the plaintiff will decide how you should pay.
- You can get help to complete this form at any county court office or citizens' advice bureau.

Where to send this form

- **If you admit the claim in full**
  Send the completed form to the address shown at box (2) on the front of the summons. If there is no address in box (2) send the form to the address in box (1).
- **If you admit only part of the claim**
  Send the form to the court at the address given on the summons, together with the white defence form (N9B).

What happens next

- **If you admit the claim in full and offer to pay**
  If the plaintiff accepts your offer, judgment will be entered and you will be sent an order telling you how and when to pay. If the plaintiff does not accept your offer, the court will fix a rate of payment based on the details you have given in this form and the plaintiff's comments. Judgment will be entered and you will be sent an order telling you how and when to pay.
- **If you admit only part of the claim**
  The court will tell you what to do next.

How much of the claim do you admit?

- ☐ I admit the full amount claimed as shown on the summons **or**
- ☐ I admit the amount of   £ _____

---

1 Personal details

Surname	
Forename	

☐ Mr   ☐ Mrs   ☐ Miss   ☐ Ms

☐ Married   ☐ Single   ☐ Other *(specify)* _____

Age _____

Address _____

Postcode _____

2 Dependants *(people you look after financially)*

Number of children in each age group

under 11 ☐   11-15 ☐   16-17 ☐   18 & over ☐

Other dependants *(give details)* _____

3 Employment

☐ I am employed as a _____

My employer is _____

Jobs other than main job *(give details)* _____

☐ I am self employed as a _____

Annual turnover is ....   £ _____

☐ I am not in arrears with my national insurance contributions, income tax and VAT

☐ I am in arrears and I owe ......   £ _____

Give details of:
(a) contracts and other work in hand
(b) any sums due for work done _____

☐ I have been unemployed for _____ years _____ months

☐ I am a pensioner

4 Bank account and savings

☐ I have a bank account

☐ The account is in credit by .....   £ _____

☐ The account is overdrawn by ..   £ _____

☐ I have a savings or building society account

The amount in the account is ......   £ _____

5 Property

I live in   ☐ my own property   ☐ lodgings
           ☐ jointly owned property ☐ council property
           ☐ rented property

N9A Form of admission and statement of means to accompany Form N1 (Order 9, rule 2)

Figure 4.5 Form N9A

6 Income

My usual take home pay *(including overtime, commission, bonuses etc)*	£	per
Income support	£	per
Child benefit(s)	£	per
Other state benefit(s)	£	per
My pension(s)	£	per
Others living in my home give me	£	per
Other income *(give details below)*		
	£	per
	£	per
	£	per
Total income	£	per

7 Expenses

(Do not include any payments made by other members of the household out of their own income)

I have regular expenses as follows :

Mortgage *(including second mortgage)*	£	per
Rent	£	per
Community charge	£	per
Gas	£	per
Electricity	£	per
Water charges	£	per
TV rental and licence	£	per
HP repayments	£	per
Mail order	£	per
Housekeeping, food, school meals	£	per
Travelling expenses	£	per
Children's clothing	£	per
Maintenance payments	£	per
Others *(not court orders or credit debts listed in boxes 9 and 10)*		
	£	per
	£	per
	£	per
Total expenses	£	per

8 Priority debts

(This section is for arrears only. Do not include regular expenses listed in box 7.)

Rent arrears		£	per
Mortgage arrears		£	per
Community charge arrears		£	per
Water charges arrears		£	per
Fuel debts:	Gas	£	per
	Electricity	£	per
	Other	£	per
Maintenance arrears		£	per
Others *(give details below)*			
		£	per
		£	per
Total priority debts		£	per

9 Court orders

Court	Case No.	£	per
Total court order instalments		£	per

Of the payments above, I am behind with payments to *(please list)*

10 Credit debts

Loans and credit card debts *(please list)*

	£	per
	£	per
	£	per

Of the payments above, I am behind with payments to *(please list)*

11 Do you wish to make an offer of payment?

- *If you take away the totals of boxes 7, 8 and 9 and the payments you are making in box 10 from the total in box 6 you will get you some some idea of the sort of sum you should offer. The offer you make should be one you can afford.*

☐ I can pay the amount admitted on

or

☐ I can pay by monthly instalments of £

12 Declaration

I declare that the details I have given above are true to the best of my knowledge

Signed   Dated

Position *(firm or company)*

Figure 4.5 (reverse)

Notice of Issue of Default Summons - fixed amount

To the plaintiff ('s solicitor)

Your summons was issued today. The defendant has 14 days from the date of service to reply to the summons. If the date of postal service is not shown on this form you will be sent a separate notice of service (Form N222).
The defendant may either
- Pay you your total claim.
- **Dispute the whole claim.** The court will send you a copy of the defence and tell you what to do next.
- **Admit that all the money is owed.** The defendant will send you form of
— admission N9A. You may then ask the court to send the defendant an order to pay you the money owed by completing the request for judgment below and returning it to the court.
- **Admit that only part of your claim is owed.** The court will send you a copy of the reply and tell you what to do next.
- **Not reply at all.** You should wait 14 days from the date of service. You may then ask the court to send the defendant an order to pay you the money owed by completing the request for judgment below and returning it to the court.

In the		
	LEEDS	
		County Court

The court office at
LEEDS COMBINED COURT CENTRE,
THE COURTHOUSE, 1 OXFORD ROW, LEEDS LS1 3BG,
is open between 10 am & 4 pm Monday to Friday
Tel:

Case Number	*Always quote this*	
Plaintiff *(including ref.)*		
Defendants		
Issue date		
Date of postal service		
Issue fee	£	

For further information please turn over

- -

Request for Judgment

- Tick and complete either A or B. Make sure that all the case details are given and that the judgment details at C are completed. Remember to sign and date the form. Your signature certifies that the information you have given is correct.
- If the defendant has given an address on the form of admission to which correspondence should be sent, which is different from the address shown on the summons, you will need to tell the court.

A ☐ **The defendant has not replied to my summons**
Complete all the judgment details at C. Decide how and when you want the defendant to pay. You can ask for the judgment to be paid by instalments or in one payment.

B ☑ **The defendant admits that all the money is owed**
Tick only **one** box below and return the completed slip to the court.

☑ **I accept the defendant's proposal for payment**
Complete all the judgment details at C. Say how the defendant intends to pay. The court will send the defendant an order to pay. You will also be sent a copy.

☐ **The defendant has not made any proposal for payment**
Complete all the judgment details at C. Say how you want the defendant to pay. You can ask for the judgment to be paid by instalments or in one payment. The court will send the defendant an order to pay. You will also be sent a copy.

☐ **I do NOT accept the defendant's proposal for payment**
Complete all the judgment details at C and say how you want the defendant to pay. Give your reasons for objecting to the defendant's offer of payment in the section overleaf. Return this slip to the court **together with the defendant's admission** N9A (or a copy). The court will fix a rate of payment and send the defendant an order to pay. You will also be sent a copy.

I certify that the information given is correct

Signed .... Dated ....

In the	**LEEDS**	
		County Court
Case Number	*Always quote this*	
Plaintiff		
Defendant		
Plaintiff's Ref.		

C Judgment details
I would like the judgment to be paid

☐ (forthwith) *only tick this box if you intend to enforce the order right away*

☑ (by instalments of £ 5 0 • 0 0   per month)

☐ (in full by   )

Amount of claim as stated in summons (including interest at date of issue)	7So	OO
Interest since date of summons (if any) .... Period 4 DAYS.... Rate 15.. %	14	25
	43	OO
Court fees shown on summons		
Solicitor's costs (if any) on issuing summons		
Sub Total	8o7	25
Solicitor's costs (if any) on entering judgment		
Sub Total	8o7	25
Deduct amount (if any) paid since issue		
Amount payable by defendant	8o7	25

N205A Notice of issue (default summons) and request for judgment (Order 3, rule (2)(d)(1), Order 9 rules 3 and 6)   MCR 2649/SP 91 7/91

Figure 4.6 Completed form N205A

Judgment for Plaintiff

(acceptance of offer)

Case No.	
Always quote this	

In the

County Court

The court office is open from 10 am to 4 pm Monday to Friday

Plaintiff

Name and address for payment *(if different from above)*

Ref/Tel no.

Defendant

Telephone:

Seal

The Defendant made an offer
of (see[1] below) and the Plaintiff accepted it

It is therefore adjudged that
the Plaintiff recover against the Defendant the sum of

for debt (and interest to date of judgment)

and

for costs

amounting together to the sum of

(And the Defendant having paid the sum of)

It is ordered that the Defendant pay the sum of

to the Plaintiff

*(by instalments of[1]

for every calendar month,

* *if no sum is shown in this box, payment is due in full by the date shown.*

the first payment to reach the Plaintiff) by

Dated

―――― **Take Notice** ――――

To the Defendant

If you made an offer and the instalments shown on the judgment are not what you offered, you should write to the court office shown on this form giving your reasons why the judgment should be changed. A hearing will be arranged and you will be told when to come to court. If this judgment is not from your local county court, it will automatically be transferred to that court for hearing.

If you do not pay in accordance with this order your goods may be removed and sold or other enforcement proceedings may be taken against you. If your circumstances change and you cannot pay, ask at the court office about what you can do.

This judgment has been registered in the Register of County Court Judgments. **This may make it difficult for you to get credit.**

When the money is paid in full (including any interest*) you can ask the court to mark the entry in the register as satisfied and for a certificate proving payment. You will have to provide proof and pay a fee. **If you pay in full within one month of judgment the entry will be removed.**

*If judgment is for more than £5,000, the plaintiff may be entitled to interest.

N30(1) Judgment for Plaintiff on acceptance of offer (Order 22, rule 1(1)).

―――― **How to Pay** ――――

● **PAYMENT(S) MUST BE MADE to the person named at the address for payment quoting their reference and the court case number.**

● **DO NOT bring or send payments to the court. THEY WILL NOT BE ACCEPTED.**

● You should allow <u>at least</u> 4 days for your payment to reach the Plaintiff or his representative.

● Make sure that you keep records and can account for all payments made. Proof may be required if there is any disagreement. It is not safe to send cash unless you use registered post.

● A leaflet giving further advice about payment can be obtained from the court.

● If you need more information you should contact the Plaintiff or his representative.

Figure 4.7 Judgment on acceptance of offer

Judgment for Plaintiff
(determination)

Plaintiff	Case No.
	Always quote this
	In the
	County Court
	The court office is open from 10 am to 4 pm Monday to Friday

Name and address for payment
(if different from above)

Telephone

Ref/Tel no.

Seal

Defendant

The court having considered the defendant's form of admission and the plaintiff's objections

It is adjudged that the plaintiff recover against the defendant the sum of ____ for debt (and interest to date of judgment)

and ____ for costs

amounting together to the sum of ____

(And the defendant having paid the sum of)

It is ordered that the defendant pay the sum of ____ to the plaintiff

* *if no sum is shown in this box, payment is due in full by the date shown*

* (by instalments of ____ for every calendar month,

the first payment to reach the plaintiff) by ____

Dated ____

If you (either the plaintiff or the defendant) object to the payment rate fixed by the court, you must write to the court with your reasons. You have 16 days from the date of the postmark to do this. A hearing will be arranged and you will both be told when to come to court. If this judgment is not from the defendant's local court, it will automatically be transferred to that court for the hearing.

——— Take Notice ———

To the defendant

If you do not pay in accordance with this order your goods may be removed and sold or other enforcement proceedings may be taken against you. If your circumstances change and you cannot pay, ask at the court office about what you can do.

This judgment has been registered in the Register of County Court Judgments. This may make it difficult for you to get credit. When the money is paid in full (including any interest*) you can ask the court to mark the entry in the register as satisfied and for a certificate proving payment. You will have to provide proof and pay a fee. If you pay in full within one month of judgment the entry will be removed.

*If the judgment is for more than £5000, the plaintiff may be entitled to interest.

——— How to Pay ———

- PAYMENT(S) MUST BE MADE to the person named at the address for payment quoting their reference and the court case number.
- DO NOT bring or send payments to the court. THEY WILL NOT BE ACCEPTED.
- You should allow at least 4 days for your payment to reach the plaintiff or his representative.
- Make sure that you keep records and can account for all payments made. Proof may be required if there is any disagreement. It is not safe to send cash unless you use registered post.
- A leaflet giving further advice about payment can be obtained from the court.
- If you need more information you should contact the plaintiff or his representative.

N30(2) Judgment for plaintiff (determination without hearing) (Order22, rule 1(1))

Figure 4.8 Order for payment

Chapter 5

Disputes, Defences and Counterclaims

The Form N9B (Figure 5.1) enables the defendant to dispute the plaintiff's claim. Section 3 enables the defendant to claim that the debt has already been paid.

Note that the defendant is required to state the amount paid, and the date and method of payment. The defendant sends the form to the court, which will make a copy of it and send it to the plaintiff. If the plaintiff agrees that payment has been made, the matter will go no further.

If the plaintiff denies that payment has been made, the action will then be transferred to the defendant's court for a hearing.

Note that Section 3 refers to payment "before the summons was issued". If payment was made *before* the summons was issued, the plaintiff is not entitled to recover the court fee or interest. Conversely, if payment was made after the issue of the summons, the plaintiff is entitled to pursue the payment of the court fee and interest. If, however, the defendant disputes liability for the court fee and interest, there will be a hearing, when the district judge will decide the issue.

In respect of any defence other than one in which the defendant alleges that the debt has been paid the court will:

(a) send a copy of the defence to the plaintiff and
(b) transfer the matter to the defendant's court for hearing.

Defence

The defence is set out in Section 4 of Form N9B. If the defendant disputes liability, the matter must be resolved by a hearing. Defences will obviously vary in content but frequent examples are:

1. I do not owe the money.
2. I did not order the goods (or services).
3. The price I was quoted was £x not £xx.
4. The goods were not what I ordered and in any case they were broken on delivery.
5. I think I have been overcharged. The work only took about fifteen minutes.

Other defences may be more complex or technical. The plaintiff must consider what is said and decide what facts and documents will support the claim and deal with the allegations made in the defence.

When a defence is delivered the court will send a copy to the plaintiff. If the claim is for £1000 or less, the court will automatically refer the case to "informal arbitration". This is a hearing before the district judge, in a private office (not in public). When referring the case to informal arbitration the court may:

(a) fix a date for a "pre-trial review" or
(b) issue "automatic directions" and direct that once its directions have been complied with a date will be fixed for a hearing or
(c) issue "automatic directions" and fix a date for the hearing.

A pre-trial review

This is a preliminary hearing when the district judge considers the allegations in the claim and in the defence and tells the parties what needs to be done to get the case ready for a hearing.

He or she may direct that witness statements be filed with the court (that the parties send copies of their documents to each other and to the court). The intention is to ensure that everything is in order and all documents lodged so that, on the date fixed for the hearing, the case is properly prepared and ready to be dealt with:

the court's time is not wasted and decisions are made as fast as the system allows.

Automatic directions

Instead of fixing a date for a pre-trial review, the court may issue automatic directions. This is done in written form and different courts may use different forms of direction. By this method the court tells the parties what must be done and fixes time limits. Examples of the sort of documents the courts can use are shown in Figures 5.2 and 5.3.

It is important that the parties appreciate that these documents are orders of the court and they must be strictly complied with. Failure to do so within the time limits imposed can result in the claim or the defence being dismissed and the defaulting party may be ordered to pay its opponent's costs (travel expenses, etc). Thus, it is essential that time limits are strictly complied with and that the parties *attend* at the dates and times fixed.

If the parties agree, there is provision for the district judge to decide the matter on the documents and witness statements filed without the need for those involved actually to attend.

The decision made by the district judge on an informal arbitration, whether witnesses attend or not, is final and there are virtually no circumstances in which a decision involving a trade debt can be challenged by any form of appeal.

Defended claims over £1000

The district judge has power to determine claims involving sums up to £5000. Such claims may, with the consent of both parties or by order of the court be dealt with by informal arbitration. Alternatively, the matter may be dealt with by a formal hearing.

Again, the court may, on receiving the defence, fix a date for a pre-trial review or issue automatic directions. It may simply send a copy of the defence to the plaintiff with a note saying "We await your instructions". In doing so, the court is *not* inviting the plaintiff to enter into correspondence on the merits or defects in the defence but is, in effect, asking "Do you wish the court to fix a date?". The choice the court makes will depend on the apparent complexity of the matter.

Legal representation

What appears to the plaintiff as a reasonably simple case may become more complex if a significant defence is delivered. In such cases the plaintiff should consider whether, at this stage, to seek legal advice and help, or whether to continue conducting the case on his or her own behalf. Equally, it must be borne in mind that a judge has discretion about whether to allow an officer of a company or an employee to represent that firm on a hearing.

Thus, if the case becomes complex the district judge, on the pre-trial review, may direct that the company must be legally represented on the hearing of the case. Alternatively, to avoid delay and embarrassment on a hearing, the representative of the company should, on the pre-trial review, ask whether the company must be legally represented.

Regardless of whether the plaintiff conducts his or her own case to a conclusion or decides to instruct solicitors, it is necessary to understand some basic rules relating to defended claims.

Pleading

This is the name given to the documents in which the parties set out their case. Thus, the particulars of the claim on the summons are a "pleading".

The defence is also a "pleading". These documents set out the facts the parties rely on.

In many county court actions there will simply be a summons and a defence. However, a defence may make allegations against the plaintiff and in such circumstances he or she must consider these allegations carefully, and decide what evidence is available to refute them and whether the allegations require an answer.

As a basic rule, if the defence comprises a denial of liability then, as no specific allegations are made against the plaintiff, there is nothing to answer. If, however, allegations are made against the plaintiff they need to be answered. The answer is put in the form of a "Reply".

Reply

There is no pre-printed form for this. The points the plaintiff wishes to dispute are set out on plain white A4 paper (not the plaintiff's letterhead), headed in the action. The document is entitled "Reply" and it sets out the facts.

For example, the plaintiff claims £250 — "the cost of advertising". Up to now, the defendant has ignored all requests for payment. However, on being served with a summons he delivers a defence saying "I do not owe the plaintiff any money". That is a simple denial of liability; no allegations are made against the plaintiff and so no Reply is needed.

But suppose the defendant put in a slightly different wording: "I do not owe the plaintiff any money. He got my name wrong in the advertisement". Here, the defendant is denying liability and seeking to justify that by alleging that the advertisement contained a mistake. The plaintiff should deal with that allegation by preparing a reply. (An example of such a Reply is shown in Figure 5.4.) This sets out the facts which the plaintiff relies on to refute the allegations made by the defendant.

The plaintiff sends a copy of the Reply to the defendant and to the court. In this way the areas of dispute are being defined and the issues in that dispute are being clarified.

Counterclaims

When the plaintiff issues a summons the claim is outlined. The defendant has the opportunity to dispute that claim by delivering a defence. The defendant also has the opportunity to make a claim against the plaintiff — a counterclaim. Form N9B (Figure 5.1) Section 5 is the document on which the defendant sets out the counterclaim.

Using the example of the claim for £250 (the cost of advertising) the defendant said: "I do not owe the plaintiff any money. He got my name wrong in the advertisement". It was necessary for the plaintiff to Reply (Figure 5.3).

Suppose the same defendant had gone on to complete Section 5 on Form N9B by writing that he counterclaims £2500 on the grounds "Because they got my name wrong I did not get the business I should have got and I claim damages of £2500 for loss of business". That is a claim for £2500 *against* the plaintiffs and it must be dealt with.

The plaintiff may feel that it is not worth proceeding but cannot, of course, stop the defendant from proceeding with the counterclaim.

Further, the plaintiff has 14 days to deal with the counterclaim. If it is not dealt with then the defendant may apply for judgment in default.

Thus, the plaintiff must reply to the defence and *defend* the counter-claim. Again, there is no pre-printed form for this; the facts are simply set out in a document headed in the action and entitled "Reply and Defence to Counterclaim". (An example, dealing with the advertising case counterclaim is in Figure 5.5.)

In this document the plaintiff sets out the facts, denies the counter-claim and puts the defendant on notice that he must prove his claim for £2500.

The pleadings define the case each party to the action is putting forward. The parties are entitled to know exactly what is being alleged against them.

In the particulars of the claim on the summons the plaintiff sets out the value of the claim, what it is for and how it is calculated (see Figure 3.3). A defendant, on reading that, knows exactly what the claim is about.

Further and better particulars

Vague allegations need to be clarified and that clarification can be obtained by asking for "further and better particulars". In effect, the party making that request is asking the other party to be specific — to say exactly what he or she means. An example will clarify the point.

The plaintiff claims a sum of money in respect of goods sold and delivered. The defendant puts in a defence saying:

> The plaintiff did deliver some goods. Some were broken, others were defective and most could not be used.
>
> I contacted the plaintiff about this three times. He said he would put it right. He never did.

Here, there are some apparently serious allegations against the plain-tiff. But they are vague and thus difficult for the plaintiff to deal with adequately.

To enable him to deal with these points, the plaintiff needs to know:

1. How many of the goods were broken?
2. How many were defective?
3. What was the defect?
4. If "most could not be used", were any used?
5. How many?
6. When and how did the defendant contact the plaintiff?
7. Did he write or telephone? Has he got copies of his letters? Who did he speak to? What was said?

The plaintiff needs this information in order to investigate the allegations made and respond to them. To obtain it, the plaintiff prepares a "request for further and better particulars of the defence". Again, there is no set form — the request should be typed on plain white A4 and a copy sent to the defendant and to the court.

In making the request the plaintiff can stipulate a time limit (a reasonable one) within which the defendant must deliver those particulars in writing.

If the defendant does not provide them, the plaintiff may apply to the court (on a pre-trial review or by application) for an order that the defendant must provide those particulars. If the court accepts that the plaintiff needs to have the requested information, it can make an order that the defendant should deliver them "or be debarred from defending". In other words, if the defendant does not give the particulars within a time limit fixed by the court, he or she will not be allowed to continue with the defence. Judgment will then be given for the plaintiff.

An example of a request for further and better particulars based on the questions above is shown in Figure 5.6. The plaintiff sends one copy of the request to the defendant and one copy to the court.

When complex defences or counterclaims are delivered the plaintiff should consider them carefully and, where appropriate, seek legal advice. A solicitor will always be prepared to take over the conduct of the case but it is important to contact the chosen person in good time. Plaintiffs cannot expect to be able to pass the papers to a solicitor a day before a hearing and get immediate attention.

When actions are transferred to the defendant's court for hearing it is sensible to instruct a solicitor in the locality of that court. A solicitor local to the plaintiff will, in most cases, instruct a solicitor in the court district to attend. There is no reason why the plaintiff should not do this personally.

Checklist — dealing with disputes, defences and counterclaims

(a) *Defendant claims debt has been paid.*
Confirm payment or non-payment to the court. If payment is disputed the case will be transferred to the defendant's court for hearing.

(b) *Defendant disputes liability.*
Consider the defence and need for a reply or request for particulars. Comply with the order for directions. The hearing will be in the defendant's court. Claims of £1000 or less go to arbitration. Is the case suitable for a decision on written statements?

(c) *The defendant disputes liability and delivers a counterclaim.*
Consider the allegations made and the need for a reply. File a defence to the counterclaim within 14 days of its delivery.

(d) *Directions for trial.*
Always comply strictly with directions given by the court and the time limits imposed.

(e) *Hearings.*
Attend at the date and time fixed by the court.

(f) *Seeking legal advice.*
When necessary seek advice *promptly*. Give the chosen solicitor as much notice of hearing dates as possible.

Defence and Counterclaim

When to fill in this form

- Only fill in this form if you wish to dispute all or part of the claim **and/or** make a claim against the plaintiff (counterclaim).

How to fill in this form

- Please check that the correct case details are shown on this form. You must ensure that all the boxes at the top right of this form are completed. You can obtain the correct names and numbers from the summons. The court cannot trace your case without this information.

- Follow the instructions given in each section. Tick the correct boxes and give the other details asked for.

- If you wish only to make a claim against the plaintiff (counterclaim) go to section 5.

- Complete and sign section 6 before returning this form.

Where to send this form

- Send or take this form immediately to the court office at the address shown above.

- If you admit part of the claim and you are asking for time to pay, you will also need to fill in the blue admission form (N9A) and send **both** reply forms to the court.

- Keep the summons and a copy of this defence; you may need them.

Legal Aid

- You may be entitled to legal aid. Ask about the legal aid scheme at any county court office, citizen's advice bureau, legal advice centre or firm of solicitors displaying the legal aid sign. **Legal Aid**

What happens next

- If you complete box 3 on this form, the court will ask the plaintiff to confirm that he has received payment. If he tells the court that you have not paid, the court will tell you what you should do.

- If you complete box 4 or 5, the court will tell you what you should do.

- If the summons is not from your local county court, it will automatically be transferred to your local court.

1 How much of the claim do you dispute ?

☐ I dispute the full amount claimed *(go to section 2)*

or

☐ I admit the amount of £ [   ] and I dispute the balance

If you dispute only part of the claim you must **either**:

- pay the amount admitted to the person named at the address for payment in box (2) on the front of the summons or if there is no address in box (2), send the money to the address in box (1) (see How to Pay on the back of the summons). Then send this defence to the court.

or

- complete the blue admission form and send it to the court with this defence.

Tick whichever applies

☐ I paid the amount admitted on [   ]

or

☐ I enclose the completed form of admission

(go to section 2)

In the

[   ] **County Court**

Case Number *Always quote this* [   ]

Plaintiff *(including ref.)*

Defendant

The court office is open from 10am to 4pm Monday to Friday

2 Arbitration under the small claims procedure

- This involves an informal hearing taking place in private instead of a formal trial held in public.

- If you defend a claim for £1000 or less it will be referred to arbitration automatically unless you apply to the court. Your local court office can give you more details.

- The decision of the arbitrator is final. There are only very limited circumstances in which the court can set aside an arbitration decision.

- If the claim is for more than £1000 it can still go to arbitration if:

  (a) You and the plaintiff agree. (He may indicate his agreement in his particulars of claim.) **or**

  (b) The court orders it (where only one party applies)

  ☐ Tick here if the claim is for more than £1000 and you would like it to be dealt with in this way.

  (go on to section 3)

3 Do you dispute this claim because you have already paid it ? *Tick whichever applies*

☐ No *(go to section 4)*

☐ Yes I paid £ [   ] to the plaintiff

on [   ] *(before the summons was issued)*

Give details of where and how you paid it in the box below *(then go to section 6)*

NB Form of defence and counterclaim to accompany Form N1 (Order 9, rule 2)

Figure 5.1 Form N9B

Case No. [   ]

4 If you dispute the claim for reasons other than payment, what are your reasons ?

Use the box below to give full details. *(If you need to continue on a separate sheet, put the case number in the top right hand corner.)*

**5 If you wish to make a claim
   against the plaintiff (counterclaim)**

If your claim is for a specific sum of money,
how much are you claiming? £ [   ]

- If your claim against the plaintiff is for
  more than the plaintiff's claim against you,
  you may have to pay a fee. Ask at your
  local court office whether a fee is payable.

- You may not be able to make a
  counterclaim where the plaintiff is the
  Crown (e.g. a Government Department).
  Ask at your local county court office for
  further information.

**What are your reasons for making the
counterclaim?**

- Use the box opposite to give full details.
  *(If you need to continue on a separate sheet, put
  the case number in the top right hand corner.)*

(go on to section 6)

6 Signed
*(To be signed by you
or by your solicitor)*

Position
*(firm or
company)*

**Give an
address to
which notices
about this case
can be sent to
you**

Dated

Postcode [   ]

Figure 5.1 (reverse)

CASE NO:

IN THE   BOURNEMOUTH   COUNTY COURT

BETWEEN   PLAINTIFF

    and   DEFENDANT

TO   Plaintiff and Defendant:

The District Judge has ordered that this case be referred to
Arbitration.
Before the Arbitration takes place, however, the District Judge has
ordered that within 28 days of today's date:

(1)   You send to the Court <u>and</u> to your opponent a full statement
      of your evidence and the statement of any witnesses you intend
      to come to the Arbitration.

(2)   You send to the court <u>and</u> to your opponent copies of any
      invoices, accounts, medical reports, police statements and
      any other documents which relate to your case [please note
      that if your case involves personal injury, a medical report
      must be filed by the Plaintiff if one was not included with
      the summons].

(3)   You send to the Court <u>and</u> to your opponent copies of any
      plans or photographs which may be relevant to the case.

(4)   Application for any other directions must be made within
      the time stated, i.e. 28 days from today, on appointment
      before the District Judge which your opponent may be
      allowed to attend.

Once these orders have been complied with the Court will give a date
and time to the parties for the hearing of the Arbitration which
you and your opponent, together with any witness whose statements
have been filed, must attend.

If you and your opponent agree, the matter may be decided on the
written evidence filed and without parties attendance. If you wish
to take advantage of this suggestion please see para. 5 on form
attached.

N.B.   It is stressed that this is an Order of the Court, and failure
       to comply may allow your opponent to succeed in the case
       unopposed. Also, you may have to pay your opponent's costs
       if the District Judge considers that you have behaved
       unreasonably in your conduct of this action.

Figure 5.2 Form of automatic directions

CASE NO:

(B)

NOTICE FOR FILING EVIDENCE

AND

REQUEST FOR ARBITRATION

IN THE   BOURNEMOUTH   COUNTY COURT

BETWEEN   PLAINTIFF

    and   DEFENDANT

Take notice that you must complete this form and attach it to your statements of evidence and other documents filed at Court [a copy of the form has also been sent to your opponent]. When the Court receives the completed form from both sides, a date for the Arbitration will be given or, if requested by both parties, the case may be decided by the District Judge without the parties attending.

You are reminded that you must send to the Court and to your opponent full statements of evidence and copy supporting documents to enable the case to be tried. Failure to do this without good excuse, which causes delay or inconvenience on the day of the Arbitration, will be considered unreasonable conduct and may result in an award of costs against the offending party.

You must complete the statements below and sign the forms where indicated

(Tick YES or NO box next to each statement)   YES   NO

(1) I enclose [   ]* statements of evidence which constitute my case in these proceedings.
         *[state number]

(2) I enclose [   ]* documents in support of my case.
(a)   *[state number]

(b) I have no supporting documents to file.

(3) I certify I have sent my opponent copies of all papers referred to in (1) and (2) above.

(4) I request this case to be listed for Arbitration.

(5) I request that this case be decided on the written evidence only and without the parties attendance [this will be done only if both parties agree and the District Judge so orders].

Dated ....   Signed ....

Figure 5.2 (continued)

CASE NO. _____

.... PLAINTIFF

.... DEFENDANT

PLEASE READ THIS CAREFULLY

TAKE NOTICE that these proceedings have been referred for arbitration by the District Judge of this Court. There will be no preliminary hearing and the action will be heard and determined by the District Judge at The Courts of Justice, Edward Street, Truro on the   day of
19   at   am/pm.

The parties should attend on that date with their witnesses and bring with them any documents on which they intend to rely.

The hearing shall be informal and the strict rules of evidence shall not apply.

At the hearing the arbitrator may adopt any method of procedure which he may consider to be convenient and to afford a fair and equal opportunity to each party to present his case.

If any party does not appear at the arbitration, the arbitrator may make an award on hearing any other party to the proceedings who may be present.

Where an award has been given in the absence of a party, the arbitrator may, on that party's application, set aside the award and order a fresh hearing.

The costs of the action up to and including the entry of judgment shall be in the discretion of the arbitrator, but no solicitors' costs shall be allowed except for the costs stated on the summons, the costs of enforcing the award and such costs as are certified by the arbitrator to have been incurred through the unreasonable conduct of the opposite party in relation to the case.

If you object to the reference to arbitration, or to any of the terms, you may apply to the reference to be rescinded or for the terms to be varied, stating in either case the ground of your application.

Alternatively the District Judge may, at the hearing referred to above, indicate that he is considering rescinding the reference to arbitration himself. In those circumstances the arbitration will not take place on that day. The Rules provide for another hearing date and for representations to be made on that day if either of the parties objects to rescission of the reference to arbitration.

THIS IS THE ORDER MADE BY THE COURT TO MAKE SURE THAT THE ACTION IS TRIED JUSTLY, SWIFTLY AND ECONOMICALLY.

Within 14 days from the date of this order the Plaintiff and the Defendant shall send to each other and lodge with the Court a copy of every document upon which they wish to rely at the hearing and shall not be permitted to produce at the hearing any document not so served without leave of the District Judge.

Figure 5.3 Automatic directions – alternative form

In cases which involve technical matters (e.g. disputes over motor cars, garage repairs or faulty goods) if either party obtains a written report or opinion a copy must be sent immediately to the other party so that he has an opportunity to obtain a written report or opinion himself. Copies of any such reports must also be lodged with the Court not less than three days before the hearing. In motor accident claims photographs of the scene of the accident or a plan should also be obtained and service as already mentioned.

No party shall produce at the hearing any document in the two preceding paragraphs unless these directions have been complied with.

Any party who fails to comply with the provisions of the aforementioned paragraphs of this order may be ordered to bear his own expenses and/or to pay any of the other party's expenses which have been wasted.

ADJOURNMENTS: It is in the interest of both parties for this dispute to be resolved as quickly as possible, but if you or any of your witnesses have genuine prior commitments which make it impossible to attend Court on the date shown you should write to the Chief Clerk immediately to ask for an adjournment. Please state your reasons and confirm any dates on which it is impossible for you to attend. If your request is made within 14 days of the date of this notice, then the application will normally be dealt with in correspondence by the Court without either party having to attend. After those 14 days if you need to ask for an adjournment you should first ask the other party to consent. If he agrees then both parties must write to the Court to confirm their agreement and confirm any dates to be avoided when fixing the date of the adjourned hearing. If the other party does not agree then you must come to the Court office immediately to obtain the necessary forms of application to request an order from the Court and attend the hearing of that application.

If either party does not attend the hearing of the action then the District Judge may still proceed to hear the case and give judgment.

YOU MAY FIND THE FOLLOWING INFORMATION OF ASSISTANCE:–

Prior to the hearing you should think carefully as to what is the exact argument between the parties.

If the case proves to be above average in length or complexity, then it is a possibility that it will not be conducted on the date in this notice and you will then have to return on another occasion.

If you think that the arbitrator should inspect the subject matter of the dispute, (e.g. a fitted carpet or decorations), you should apply to the Court before the date given for the arbitration to be held at the place where the subject matter is, but on another day. The Registrar may make a direction accordingly.

DATED: DISTRICT JUDGE

Figure 5.3 (continued)

In the [court name] County Court

Between: Case No. _____

A. Creditor Limited

Plaintiffs

and

Joseph Debtor

Defendant

REPLY

1. It is denied that the Defendant's name was incorrect in the advertisement.

2. The name inserted in the advertisement was identical to that shown in the advertising proof signed by the Defendant on _____

Dated _____

To The Court   Signed _____

And To The Defendant   For and on behalf of the
                                Plaintiffs whose address
                                for service is _____

                                _____

Figure 5.4 Example of a reply

In the [court name] County Court

Between: Case No. _____

A. Creditor Limited

Plaintiffs

and

Joseph Debtor

Defendant

Reply and Defence to Counterclaim

REPLY

1. It is denied that the Defendant's name was incorrect in the advertisement.

2. The name inserted in the advertisement was identical to that shown in the advertising proof signed by the Defendant on _____

Defence to Counterclaim

3. The Plaintiffs repeat paragraphs 1 and 2 of the Reply.

4. The Plaintiffs deny that the Defendant suffered any loss or damage and put the Defendant to strict proof.

Dated _____

To The Court   Signed _____

And To The Defendant   For and on behalf of the
                                      Plaintiffs whose address
                                      for service is_____
                                      _____

Figure 5.5 Example of a reply and defence to counterclaim

In the [name of court] County Court

Case No. _____

Between:

A. Creditor Limited

Plaintiffs

and

Joseph Debtor

Defendant

Request for Further and Better Particulars
of the Defence

The Plaintiffs require the Defendant, within 14 days of the date
hereof to deliver in writing, to them, the following further and better
Particulars of the Defence:

1. Of "some were broken" specify how many of the goods are alleged
   to have been broken.
2. Of "some were defective" specify:
   (i)   How many of the goods are alleged to have been defective.
   (ii) Specify the alleged defect in each case.
3. Of "most could not be used" specify:
   (i)   How many could not be used.
   (ii) How many were used.
4. Of "I contacted the Plaintiffs about this three times", specify how
   such contact is alleged to have been made. If by telephone, specify:
   (i)   Who the Defendant spoke to as representing the Plaintiffs.
   (ii) The date of each telephone conversation.
   (iii) The facts relied on to support the allegation that the
         Plaintiffs "said they would put it right". If contact was
         by letter the Defendant is required to produce copies of the
         letters. If contact was by any other means, specify the
         means.

Dated the   day of   19

To the Court   Signed _____

And To the Defendant   For and on Behalf of the
                                Plaintiffs whose address
                                for service is _____

Figure 5.6 Example of a request for further and better particulars

Chapter 6

Hearings

There are three types of hearing that plaintiffs may have to deal with:

(a) disposal
(b) arbitration
(c) trial.

Disposal hearing

As outlined in Chapter 4, a disposal is a hearing before the district judge. It arises when the defendant admits the debt but makes an offer to pay which is not accepted by the plaintiff.

The debt itself is not in dispute and the only question to be decided is how much per week or per month the defendant should pay.

The defendant sets out the offer on Form N9A (Figure 4.5). If the plaintiff rejects that offer the matter will be reviewed by a court official who will fix the amount of repayment; either party to the action can object to that decision.

If an objection is made the matter will be transferred to the defendant's court for a disposal hearing before the district judge.

The plaintiff and the defendant will be given notice of the date, time and place of the hearing. The plaintiff may wish to instruct a local firm of solicitors to attend on his or her behalf. In such circum- stances it will not be necessary for the plaintiff to attend as well. The claim does not need to be *proved* and the only issue is how much the defendant's instalments should be.

Ability to pay

In reaching a decision the district judge will consider the defendant's ability to pay. That decision must depend on:

(a) information provided by the defendant on Form N9A
(b) any information the plaintiff can provide on the hearing
(c) information obtained by asking questions of the defendant on the hearing.

Information on Form N9A

The form requires the defendant to provide quite detailed information about income, assets and liabilities. The form will be sent by the defendant direct to the plaintiff.

Some defendants may make an offer but fail to complete the form as required. In such cases the plaintiff may decide to make a copy of the form and return it to the defendant indicating that it is not possible to consider the offer until the form is returned fully completed. If the form is not completed and returned within, say, ten days then the plaintiff should send the original to the court, with Form N205A, rejecting the offer.

One of the grounds for rejection would be: "The Defendant has failed to complete the details required and has ignored a letter from the Plaintiffs dated _____ requesting its completion and return".

The plaintiff can indicate on Form N205A how he or she wishes to be paid. The court official will then make an appropriate order. If either party objects to that decision a disposal date can be fixed.

If the Form N9A is completed, the plaintiff should consider the information provided and focus on any particular matters he or she wishes to comment on or question on the hearing.

Information the plaintiff can provide

When granting credit, the plaintiff should have obtained some information about the defendant's creditworthiness. It is necessary to compare the information the defendant provided at the time the credit was granted with that provided on Form N9A. Has anything changed? What other information can the plaintiff provide about the defendant's current position?

Information obtained by questioning the defendant on the hearing

The plaintiff or solicitor has the opportunity, on the hearing, to ask the defendant questions. Obviously, the intention is to demonstrate that the defendant can afford to pay more. Whilst the opportunity to "cross examine" the defendant may seem to open up an exciting prospect, plaintiffs must realise the scope of the hearing.

The court is seeking to make an order that the defendant can comply with, not to impose punishment. Effective cross examination must depend on what the questioner *knows* about the defendant.

For example, a series of useful questions might be:

Plaintiff : "You said, on opening your account that you banked at XY Bank."

Defendant : "I may have done."

Plaintiff : "In your admission form you say you have no bank account."

Defendant : "That's right."

Plaintiff : "Would it surprise you to know that last week XY Bank said, on a reference of £1000 — 'Will prove good for your figure'?"

So, in this example the plaintiff has made some enquiries and has information to build on. What is totally unhelpful is an unsupported attack on the defendant, for example accusing him or her of lying about the ability to pay.

When considering offers and the need for a disposal hearing, plaintiffs should take a *commercial* view of the situation. If the debt is going to be repaid over a reasonable period then it is worth accepting the offer. To reject it means further delay whilst the court official makes a determination. If either party objects to that decision, there will be further delay until a date for disposal is fixed.

First payment

The first payment will usually be ordered to be made one month after the hearing.

Accepting the offer or accepting the decision of the court official means obtaining an order for payment — a judgment — without the need for a hearing. Bearing in mind that a hearing will take place in the *defendant's* court, there is also the question of cost to be considered (the plaintiff's representative travelling to the court, the cost of instructing solicitors to attend when necessary). Disposal hearings will take place in the office of the district judge, in private.

Arbitration

Claims of £1000 or less which are defended will be dealt with by arbitration. As outlined in Chapter 5, this is an informal hearing which takes place before the district judge, in private in his or her office.

Once a defence is delivered then the court may:

(a) give automatic directions or
(b) fix a pre-trial review or
(c) issue automatic directions and fix a date for hearing.

These options are totally at the discretion of the court and are described in Chapter 5.

It is likely that in arbitration matters most courts will issue automatic directions and fix dates. Further, in many cases these automatic directions will, in future, require the parties to file and exchange written statements of witnesses.

A further development will be a greater use of the provision enabling the district judge to determine the issue on the statements and documents lodged without the need for attendance by the parties.

Plaintiffs must ensure that they comply strictly with directions given by the court and that they attend on the dates and times fixed.

Delays

Claims do take time to go through the court system. Many people complain of "the law's delays". Some delays are inherent in the system, others are caused by the parties involved.

For example, a date is fixed and a few days before the hearing the plaintiff may write to the court saying that a witness will be unable to attend, etc, and ask for another date. The time of the district judge is therefore wasted if there is no other case that can be fitted in in the time available and delays occur.

In future, when dates are fixed they will not be changed without a good and valid reason; if parties fail to attend the case will be dealt with in their absence.

Attendance

To emphasise the importance of attendance, s. 12 of the **Courts and Legal Services Act 1990** deals with the situation where:

> . . . an appointment has been fixed for any hearing in the High Court or in any County Court, but a party to the proceedings:
>
> a) Has failed to appear; or
> b) Has failed to give the court due notice of his desire to cancel the hearing or of his inability to appear at it.
>
> The Court may summon the party concerned, or the person conducting the proceedings on his behalf, to explain his failure.

The court has the power to impose a fine on the person in default.

Plaintiffs attending arbitration hearings should ensure that the relevant witnesses appear and that they have with them all the documents they need to support their case. They must also be prepared to deal with the allegations raised by the defence.

The plaintiff needs to begin by proving the claim. The district judge may ask questions and consider the documents. The defendant will then be asked to make any points and produce witnesses to support the defence.

The judge will then make a decision (judgment) and the court will draw it up and send a copy to the plaintiff and the defendant.

As outlined in Chapter 5, claims up to £5000 *may*, with the consent of both parties, be dealt with by arbitration. Some plaintiffs include a request for such arbitration in their particulars of claim by adding a paragraph "In the event of a Defence being delivered the Plaintiffs request that the matter be dealt with by Arbitration".

The idea of a simple, informal way of dealing with disputes is appealing. But plaintiffs should bear in mind certain drawbacks to the arbitration process:

1. If the plaintiff instructs a solicitor to attend, the court will not,

even if the plaintiff "wins" the case, order the defendant to pay
the plaintiff's solicitor's costs of attending the hearing.
2. The rights of appeal against a decision on arbitration are severely
   limited.
3. The plaintiff will not be able to use the summary judgment
   procedure (see Chapter 8) if he or she has opted for arbitration.

Nevertheless, plaintiffs who do make use of the arbitration process
will secure a reasonably fast, inexpensive and informal decision.

One area of doubt has been clarified as a result of the **Courts and
Legal Services Act 1990**. Prior to that Act there was some doubt as
to whether a counterclaim over £1000 could be dealt with by arbitration. (In other words, the plaintiff's claim is £750 (so if defended
qualifies for arbitration) but the defendant not only defends but
counterclaims £1500.) That does not now preclude arbitration and the
matter may still be dealt with by that process.

Trials

Matters not dealt with by arbitration are dealt with by a "trial" of
the action. The district judge has the power to deal with claims up
to £5000; claims of a major nature, perhaps involving an important
point of law, may be referred to a judge; claims over £5000 *will* be
referred to a judge.

Such claims are referred to as being "in open court" which simply
means that they are held in a court to which the public may be
admitted.

Plaintiffs conducting their own actions must have regard to the
rules relating to rights of audience. On a defended action the judge
has discretion as to whether a limited company can be represented
by an officer or employee.

Rights of audience

The **Courts and Legal Services Act 1990**, s. 27, deals with rights of
audience and directs:

1) The question whether a person has a right of audience before a Court,
   or in relation to any proceedings, shall be determined solely in accordance with the provisions of this part.

2) A person shall have a right of audience before a Court in relation to any proceedings only in the following cases:

a) Where:

    i) He has a right of audience before that Court in relation to those proceedings granted by the appropriate authorised body; and

    ii) That body's qualification regulations and rules of Conduct have been approved for the purposes of this section, in relation to the granting of that right;

b) Where paragraph (a) does not apply but he has a right of audience before that Court in relation to those proceedings granted by or under any enactment;

c) Where paragraph (a) does not apply but he has a right of audience granted by that Court in relation to those proceedings;

d) Where he is a party to those proceedings and would have had a right of audience, in his capacity as such a party, if this Act had not been passed; or

e) Where:

    i) He is employed (whether wholly or in part), or is otherwise engaged, to assist in the conduct of litigation and is doing so under instructions given (either generally or in relation to the proceedings) by a qualified litigator; and

    ii) The proceedings are being heard in chambers in the High Court or a County Court and are not reserved family proceedings.

This, in effect, means that a judge may allow an officer or employee of a limited company to conduct a case but could direct that the plaintiffs (being a limited company) *must* be legally represented.

Clearly, if the plaintiff is facing a complicated defended action, to be heard before a judge in open court, it is sensible to seek legal representation in any event.

On a trial in open court witnesses must attend to give their evidence in person.

The careful and detailed preparation of the documents and oral evidence is an essential element of success in such cases. Again, where considerable sums are involved and complex issues are raised, legal representation makes sense.

Cost

Another important issue to consider when facing a trial in open court is cost. Costs in litigation are high and are not easy to control. Some solicitors deal with the "advocacy" (the presentation and argument of a case), others instruct "counsel" (a barrister).

Counsel's fees are based on their expertise, length of practice and the time spent. Able counsel charge high fees and both solicitors and counsel are paid, win or lose.

There is a general rule that the loser pays but this is at the discretion of the judge. Usually, *some* of the costs are ordered to be borne by the loser. However, the winner will have to pay some part of the costs incurred by the solicitors instructed.

Again, if the loser (say the defendant) simply *cannot* pay the debt or the costs then the plaintiffs do not recover their debt and they have to pay all their own costs. A sensible settlement is always preferable to a Pyrrhic victory. Solicitors are always conscious of the problem of cost and if they suggest a negotiated settlement it is not a sign of weakness but of practicality.

A final factor to consider in facing a trial in open court is the strength of the claim and the defence and, when it arises, the counterclaim. Even if the plaintiff is legally represented it is still his or her case and he or she will have to produce the evidence, the documents and the witnesses. (See Chapter 7 Evidence and Chapter 15 Working with Solicitors.)

Whilst it is appropriate for plaintiffs to issue their own summonses in the county court and to deal with arbitrations, judgments in default and on admission, and the enforcement of judgments, there is a time to seek expert advice. That time must be when a substantial claim raises a substantial defence and a full scale trial is indicated.

Chapter 7

Evidence

A party to an action who alleges anything as a fact must prove it by means of evidence. There are strict rules concerning evidence, designed to ensure relevancy and fairness. It is on the evidence produced by the parties that the court will determine the issue in dispute in an action. Thus, the preparation of a case for trial involves consideration of the facts, the evidence necessary to prove them and the documents that exist.

In complex cases, involving counsel, it is usual for him or her to be asked to advise, in writing, on the necessary evidence. For the purposes of this book it will suffice to deal with basic principles relating to evidence which will consist of:

(a) witnesses who give evidence and
(b) documents.

Witnesses

A witness may be required to attend and give evidence in person or, in arbitration cases, statements may be required to be lodged with the court *and* provided to the other party.

A witness may only testify to what he or she knows from his or her own knowledge, not what he or she has been told.

For example, a credit controller's evidence may relate to the opening of the account, the attempts made to collect payment and the fact that the amount shown on the summons remains unpaid. The credit controller cannot give evidence that "Our sales manager discussed the debt with the defendant who told our sales manager that . . . " That would be the sales manager's evidence. (Of course, the credit controller can give evidence about what the defendant said to him or her.) Thus, it is important for the plaintiff to ensure that the appropriate witnesses are available.

When, in arbitration cases, witness statements are to be prepared in writing there are some basic guidelines to follow:

1. The full name, private address and occupation of the witness must be given.
2. Acts, not opinions, are required and they should be set out in numbered paragraphs.
3. The facts should deal concisely with the points set out in the claim, in the defence and, when there is one, the counterclaim.
4. The statement should be signed and dated. It does not need to be countersigned by a witness to the signature.

Statements

Presentation is very important when written statements are lodged with the court. Clearly typed, well set out and well presented documents are better received than handwritten garbled statements, undated and signed with an unreadable scrawl.

An example of the format of a statement for use in an arbitration, where statements are to be lodged, is shown in Figure 7.1. As shown in that example, the statement should be prepared on plain white A4 and headed with the names of the parties and the case number.

When witnesses attend to give evidence in person they will be required to take an oath to tell the truth or to affirm if taking an oath is contrary to their religious belief or because they have no creed.

Examination of witnesses

First a witness is examined by the party calling him or her. As it is assumed that the witness will favour that party its representative must not "lead" the witness. For example, he or she cannot ask:

"Did you tell the defendant that . . . ?" but instead may ask "What did you tell the defendant?".

After this examination the other party or representative may cross examine the witness. In that situation, because it is assumed that the witness will not favour the other party, its case may be put quite forcibly and leading is permitted, eg "In fact my clients said . . . and you replied . . . didn't you?".

Witnesses may be asked to look at and explain the documents in the case.

After cross examination the witness may be re-examined by the party calling him or her in order to clarify any uncertainties. The judge may intervene to ask questions or to help to clarify certain matters.

Opinion

It is important to understand that witnesses can only testify to what they saw, heard or did. They cannot give their opinion. For example, a witness may testify that "I wrote to the defendant asking for payment and did not receive a reply. I then passed the matter for a summons to be issued". But that witness cannot say "I came to the conclusion that the defendant had no intention of paying".

Expert evidence

An obvious exception to this rule concerns expert evidence. The purpose of calling an expert in a particular field will be to get an expert's "opinion". Such witnesses are allowed to give opinions.

Relevant

There is also a rule of relevancy. This ensures that nothing is said that is not relevant to the matters in dispute. For example, it is relevant for a witness to say that written requests for payment were made and ignored but irrelevant to say that the defendant had always been a slow payer and was well known for paying at the last possible moment.

Documents

The decision in many actions turns on the documents produced by the parties. It is at this stage that the strengths or weaknesses of a party are revealed.

Obviously the plaintiff needs to ensure that he or she has all the appropriate documents to prove the case. However, as has been seen, the court will direct the parties to file a list of documents and provide copies to each other. In cases where small sums are involved, the court may simply direct that copies of all relevant documents be lodged prior to the hearing. In some cases it will direct that "lists of documents" be exchanged between the parties. ("Document" includes "paper, photographs, computer disks, films, tapes, records and compact disks" — anything, in fact, which carries information.)

It must be remembered that the obligation is to produce *all* the documents relating to the matters in dispute, not just those that prove a party's case. Thus, when a list of documents is required, all of them must be included. A form of list of documents is given in Figure 7.2 and there is provision on that list for scheduling documents which are "privileged".

Privilege

Certain documents may exist which, although they have to be listed do not have to be shown to the other party to the action.

The law of "privilege" is complex but for the purposes of this section it is sufficient to deal with the two basic types of document for which privilege can be claimed. They are:

(a) professional advice documents
(b) "without prejudice" correspondence.

Professional advice documents

A party to an action may obtain legal advice from lawyers before commencing an action, and further advice as the action proceeds. Clearly the letters and opinions created by this process may contain information that, whilst relevant to the case, are documents passing between the party and his or her legal advisers. Whilst such documents exist, and must therefore be listed, they do not have to be disclosed to the other party because advice given by lawyers to clients is private.

However, this rule is not absolute. In *Balabel v Air India* 1988, the Court of Appeal considered the question. It concluded that cases which appeared to extend total privilege to *all* solicitor/client communications were wrong. The Court of Appeal held that such privilege should only cover documents dealing with the requesting and giving of advice.

"Without prejudice" correspondence

In the course of an action or perhaps even before an action begins, attempts may be made to resolve the dispute. Obviously, such negotiations would be very difficult if a party could produce the letters used in them on a hearing. Thus letters in the course of such negotiations are marked "without prejudice" to prevent them being disclosed to the court. However, simply using the words "without prejudice" does not automatically prevent production of material in court. The simple test is whether such letters are part of a genuine attempt to negotiate a settlement.

The use of the words "without prejudice" is misunderstood and often causes confusion. The phrase should be put at the top of the letter, not within the body of the wording and, in general, should only be used in the course of negotiation. Thus, an offer by the plaintiff to accept a sum of money less than claimed, in order to dispose of a matter, should be marked "without prejudice". Then, if negotiations fail and an action goes to court, the defendant cannot produce that letter as evidence that the plaintiff agreed to settle.

However, there may be occasions when an open letter (ie one not marked "without prejudice") should be sent (see Chapter 9).

If the court directs a list of documents the form shown in Figure 7.2 should be completed. The form enables privilege to be claimed for appropriate documents. Such documents need to be separately listed but can be described as "Correspondence between the plaintiffs and their solicitors brought into existence solely for the purpose of prosecuting this action".

The parties must also deal with documents which they have had, but do not currently possess. The obvious ones are the originals of letters sent to other parties. The sender will now only have copies, the recipient will have the originals. Again, these do not need to be separately listed and the usual wording for this section is "The orig-inals of the copy letters referred to which were last in the possession of the plaintiffs on the dates which they bear, on which date they were despatched to the parties to whom they are addressed".

As neither privileged documents nor the copy documents above are listed separately, the word "various" can be inserted in the date column.

Discovery and inspection

The process of producing lists and exchanging copies of documents is known as discovery and inspection. It occurs only in defended actions and takes place when the pleadings are ended. However, if in a pleading or any affidavit filed in the course of the action a document is referred to, the opposing party is then entitled to a copy immediately.

For example if a defendant says: "The defendant will rely on a specification prepared by Bloggs dated 15th June . . . " the plaintiff is entitled to a copy of that specification because it has been used as part of the defendant's case, is alleged to be relevant and is relied on by the defendant.

Careful consideration of all the documents in the case is an essential part of preparing for a hearing. As has been stated before it is also important to provide clear clean copies for the use of the court. If the parties give the impression that they "cannot be bothered" to play their part in resolving *their* dispute, why should the court waste judicial time on it? In the case of *Davies v Eli Lilley & Co* 1987 the Master of the Rolls said:

> Litigation in this country is conducted cards face up on the table. It is designed to do a real job between opposing parties and, if the Court does not have all the relevant information, it cannot achieve this object.

Evidence in arbitration hearings

The concept of arbitration was the creation of a system for dealing with claims on the basis that:

(a) the hearing would be informal and

(b) the strict rules of evidence would not apply.

In the **Courts and Legal Services Act**, the court is given powers enabling the district judge to direct the manner in which evidence on an arbitration will be given.

Thus the district judge may order witness statements to be lodged in court and exchanged between the parties. He or she may order that all documents to be used should be exchanged and lodged prior to the hearing.

If expert witnesses are involved then the court will, following a long established procedure, direct that their statements be disclosed to the other party prior to the hearing. This process is designed to improve the prospect of sensible settlements, to ensure that cases are properly prepared and to shorten the time of hearings.

Automatic directions or orders made on a pre-trial review will clearly indicate the steps each party must take to prepare and lodge evidence.

In the   County Court.   Case No.

between

A. Creditor Limited

Plaintiffs

and

Joseph Debtor

Defendant

John Frederick Smith of 27 The Highway.

1. I am the Credit Manager of the above named Plaintiff Company and the facts set out in this statement are within my own knowledge.

2. On the   day of   1991 I received in the normal course of my work a form of Credit Application in the standard form used by my Company which was signed by Mr. J. Debtor. That document contains the basic information my Company requires from every customer who seeks to open a Credit Account and in addition on the reverse of that document the standard terms and conditions on which my Company extend credit were stipulated.

3. Subsequently invoices in respect of goods supplied to Mr. Debtor were raised in my Department and despatched to Mr. Debtor in the normal course of business. Subsequently on the   day of   1991 I spoke to Mr. Debtor pointing out that as there was a sum of £3,625 overdue for payment to my Company his Account had been placed on a credit stop and we would not be prepared to supply any further goods to him until such time as his Account was cleared.

4. Mr. Debtor agreed to send a cheque for the full amount within the course of the next three days. A cheque for that sum was duly received and presented to my Company's bank account in the normal way. On the day that the cheque was received Mr. Debtor telephoned asking me to confirm that the account was clear. I advised that we had received the cheque and that as soon as it had cleared our bank his account would be credited with the amount and we would then be in a position to supply further goods to him.

5. According to the records that I kept of my contact with all customers there were two other occasions within the next four days when Mr. Debtor contacted me by telephone asking if we were in a position to release goods. My Company's policy in such cases is not to release goods until such time as cheques are cleared.

6. I have carefully checked the records of the Company and I can say there is no record whatsoever of Mr. Debtor or anyone on his behalf subsequently placing an order for goods which was rejected. Any orders from customers who have credit accounts with the Company and any orders from new customers come to me for authorization. When an order is authorized I note the customer's records accordingly. The customer's record card for Mr. Debtor shows only a debit in respect of the goods supplied and a subsequent credit in respect of the cheque referred to above when it was duly cleared. Thereafter no orders whatsoever were placed by Mr. Debtor or by anyone on his behalf.

Dated the   day of   1991.

....
Signed.

Figure 7.1 Witness statement

List of Documents

Plaintiff

Defendant

In the		
		County Court
Case Number	Always quote this	

(1) Delete words in brackets if list is sent in response to automatic directions (O17 r11).

(2) Insert date.

The following is a list of documents which contain information about matters in dispute in this case which are or have been in my possession(1). [They are sent in response to your request dated(2)   19   .]

Schedule 1 PART I

(3) List and number here in a convenient order the documents (or bundles of documents if of the same nature, eg: invoices) in your possession which you do not object to being inspected. Give a short description of each document or bundle so that it can be identified and say if it is kept elsewhere i.e bank, solicitor.

I have in my possession the documents numbered and listed here. I do not object to you inspecting them(3).

N.265 List of documents
         O. 14, r. 1(5)

[P.T.O.

Figure 7.2 List of documents

Schedule 1 PART II

(4) List and number here, as above, the documents in your possession which you object to being inspected.

I have in my possession the documents numbered and listed here but I object to you inspecting them([4]).

(5) Say what your objections are.

I object to you inspecting these documents because([5]): —

Figure 7.2 (continued)

Schedule 2

(6) List and number here, the documents you once had in your possession but which you no longer have when this list is served. For each document listed say when it was last in your possession and where it is now.

I have had the documents numbered and listed below, but they are no longer in my possession([6]).

All the documents which are or have been in my possession and which contain information about the matters in dispute in this case are listed in Schedules 1 and 2.

(7) "Plaintiff" or "Defendant".

(8) Insert date.

Signed([7]):   Dated([8]):

Figure 7.2 (continued)

In the   County Court

Dated the   day of   19   .

                              V.

                    ════════════════════
                    ════════════════════

                    List of Documents

                    ════════════════════
                    ════════════════════

                                                    Solicitors

Solicitor's Reference:

OYEZ The Solicitors' Law Stationery Society Ltd., Oyez House,
       27 Crimscott Street, London SE1 5TS   10.90 F18207
                                                   5039202
                    County Court N265   * * * * *

Figure 7.2 (backsheet)

Chapter 8

Summary Judgment

The courts exist to resolve disputes. They do this by means of "hearing". When a defence or a defence and counterclaim is delivered, the only way the courts can deal with the matter is by arranging a hearing.

The plaintiff may have evidence in his or her file to show that there is no substance in the defence. However that evidence can only be produced on a hearing. Thus, by filing a defence a defendant can gain time.

If the claim is £1000 or less it will be dealt with by arbitration. If it exceeds £1000 but is less than £5000 then, with the consent of the parties, it may be dealt with by arbitration.

Order 9 rule 14 of the County Court Rules provides the plaintiff with a method for dealing with "time-wasting" or invalid defences. The procedure is designed to provide a quick appointment before the district judge. It also places the onus on the defendant to satisfy the district judge that he or she has a genuine dispute — a valid argument. This does not apply to arbitration cases.

If, on receiving the defence, the plaintiff wishes to use this summary judgment procedure, he or she must prepare an affidavit. This is a sworn statement of the facts, by someone authorised by the plaintiff who has knowledge of the case. The person swearing the affidavit is the "deponent". It may be necessary to produce some documents to show that the defence is invalid; these are known as "exhibits".

As an example of the way in which the summary judgment procedure works, assume that the plaintiff has claimed £2000 — the price of goods sold and delivered. Prior to the issue of proceedings the plaintiff made the usual requests for payment and, in reply to the "final demand" the debtor replied "I am waiting for a large cheque from one of my customers. As soon as I receive it I will settle your account in full". No payment is made and so the plaintiff issues a summons; he feels that there is no answer to his claim.

However, the defendant sends in a defence: "I do not owe the plaintiffs any money. I have never ordered any goods from them and they have never requested payment. If they had, I would have told them I owe them nothing".

The defendant is a liar (or an absent minded person) but the court cannot make any decision on the issue until it comes to a hearing. There may be a pre-trial review, an order for exchange of documents, and it may take some months to set a hearing date. To shorten this process, the plaintiff opts for summary judgment.

Affidavit

There is no pre-printed form for the affidavit but an example, based on the above circumstances, is shown at Figure 8.1.

Here, the deponent provides his full name and home address. In paragraph 1 he gives his occupation and confirms that he is duly authorised to make the affidavit. A company director or company secretary *is* authorised by reason of his or her office. An employee must confirm that he or she is authorised (told) to make the affidavit.

Having said, in paragraph 2, that he has read the defence, the deponent then deals with it in paragraphs 3 and 4. He "exhibits" the order placed by the defendant and the letter promising payment.

Paragraph 5 is a formal final paragraph alleging that there is no defence to the claim and asking for judgment. It stipulates Order 9 rule 14 of the County Court Rules 1981 as the basis of that application.

The documents that are exhibited should be prepared and "marked" as exhibits. This marking is done by preparing a back-sheet (Figure 8.2). Then each document is marked with its number and stapled to the back-sheet.

The affidavit and exhibits are taken by the deponent to any solicitor, or to the chief clerk of the county court. There he swears (or affirms) that he is the deponent, he confirms his signature and the truth of the facts. The standard wording is: "I swear by Almighty

God that that is my name and handwriting and the contents of my affidavit are true and those are the exhibits referred to". The solicitor or chief clerk will countersign the documents and return them to the deponent. There will be a fee payable.

Date of hearing of application

The plaintiff now needs a date for the hearing of the application. How this is obtained will depend on the course of action adopted by the court when forwarding the defence. It may have fixed a date for the pre-trial review or may simply have sent a note: "We await your instructions". If the court has fixed a date for the pre-trial review then that is the date on which the plaintiff must apply for summary judgment.

In that situation, the plaintiff writes a letter to the court, similar to Figure 8.3. The original affidavit and exhibits are enclosed, and copies sent, with a copy of the letter to the court, to the defendant.

The defendant must have seven clear days' notice of the plaintiff's application.

Notice of application

If the court adopts the course of sending a note with the defence — "We await your instructions" — the plaintiff must apply for a hearing of his or her application. He or she completes a notice of application form, Figure 8.4, (the appropriate wording to insert is shown in the example). This is sent to the court, in triplicate, together with the original affidavit and exhibits and a letter (see example in Figure 8.5).

The court will set a date and endorse it on the notice of application. It will send a copy to the plaintiff and to the defendant.

The parties attend the hearing, which takes place before the district judge. The onus is on the defendant to satisfy the judge that there is a genuine dispute between the parties and that he or she is not simply delaying the inevitable. The defendant should do this by producing an affidavit justifying the defence.

The plaintiff's approach at the hearing is on the basis of "This is our application Sir, our affidavit is on the file". They may go on to say "The defendant has not attended".

In that case the district judge may give judgment in favour of the plaintiff. This is entirely a matter for the judge who has the power to make any order he or she feels is appropriate. He or she may give judgment, or adjourn the matter to another date and direct that if the defendant does not attend on the next occasion then judgment will be given against him or her.

If the defendant attends on the first hearing he or she should produce an affidavit setting out the grounds of the defence in detail. If he or she attends but does not produce an affidavit, the district judge will usually allow him or her to say what he or she wants to in answer to the claim.

Again, the district judge has power to make any order he or she feels is appropriate in the circumstances:

(a) give judgment for the plaintiff for the full amount or
(b) give judgment for the plaintiff for part of the debt and give the defendant leave to defend the case as to the balance or
(c) decide that there is a genuine dispute that can only be determined by a full hearing.

If the district judge gives judgment for the plaintiff then the court office will draw up the judgment and, unless the defendant pays, the plaintiff is entitled to take enforcement action as soon as the judgment is drawn up (see Chapter 10 Enforcement Actions).

If the district judge feels that some money is due to the plaintiff but that there is a genuine dispute about the balance he or she may:

(a) order that the defendant pays that part of the claim to the plaintiff or
(b) order that the money be paid into the court "to abide the event".

A condition of the leave to defend may be to make the payment. Thus, the order the judge makes, which will be drawn up in the court office, may stipulate:

> The Defendant, on paying the sum of £x to the Plaintiffs (or "into the Court to abide the event") within seven days be given leave to Defend this action.
>
> In default of such payment the Plaintiffs to be at liberty to enter Judgment for the total of the claim.

Then, if the defendant does not make the payment as ordered the plaintiff may apply for judgment by completing the tear off section of Form N205A (Figure 4.1).

To abide the event

If money is paid into court "to abide the event" it simply means that it remains there until the case has been decided.

The district judge may decide that there is a genuine dispute between the parties that can only be resolved by a full hearing but in doing this he or she is *not* indicating that the plaintiff has a poor case or that the defendant has a good defence. When making decisions on summary judgment applications, the district judge has to determine whether there is an issue between the parties that can only be fairly determined by considering all the facts and evidence on a formal hearing.

Leave to defend

On giving the defendant "leave to defend" the district judge will go on to give directions for trial, telling each side what they must do to get the matter ready for a full hearing. If the defendant has not filed an affidavit, the judge may direct that he or she does so within a fixed time. He or she will also give directions about exchange of documents, witness statements and so on.

If the claim is £5000 or less the judge may direct that the matter be dealt with by arbitration.

Summary

The summary judgment procedure thus offers a fast method for dealing with what are clearly time wasting and invalid defences but it will only be practical to use it in those cases where the claim exceeds £1000 and has not been referred to arbitration.

In addition, it will not be possible to use the procedure unless the plaintiff can set out, in the affidavit, a convincing case, supported whenever possible by documentation which shows that there is no valid defence.

Because the claim is defended it will mean that the summary judgment application will take place in the defendant's court. If that involves the plaintiff in travel of some distance he or she can, of course, instruct local solicitors to attend (see Chapter 15 Working with Solicitors). On this sort of application the plaintiff need not attend; the affidavit sets out his or her case.

The example affidavit (Figure 8.1) is deliberately short. It only deals with the facts of the case, not opinions. Plaintiffs should follow this example closely; after all, they are alleging that the case is very simple and that there is no genuine defence.

If it takes ten pages to say how simple the case is, the court may decide that it cannot be that simple. The district judge will not have the time, on this sort of application, to plough through voluminous documents and long and complicated affidavits. If he or she is required to do so then the sheer volume of the documents and affidavits may tend to show that the matter is not appropriate for summary judgment.

This procedure has not been widely used in the past. However, with the increasing value of debts that will now come before the county court it may be more extensively used in the future. At best, it will give the plaintiff a faster way to judgment. At worst it will lead to the court giving directions for trial whilst defining the areas of dispute.

Checklist — summary judgment

(a) *On receipt of defence.*
   Consider its allegations and the available facts and evidence to refute them.
(b) *Good evidence is available.*
   Prepare and swear affidavit and exhibits.
(c) *Obtain date.*
   If a pre-trial review is fixed, give notice to the court and defendant of the intention to apply for summary judgment.
   If no date is fixed, complete form of notice of application.

SUGGESTED WORDING

AFFIDAVIT SUPPORTING A REQUEST FOR SUMMARY JUDGMENT

In the   County Court
                                                                    Case No.

Between   A.B. Ltd.

                                                                    Plaintiffs

                       and

                                 C.D. Ltd.

                                                                    Defendants

I (Full Names) of (Home Address) made Oath and say as follows:

1.   I am the Credit Manager to the abovenamed Plaintiffs duly authorised by
        them to make this Affidavit on their behalf. The facts herein deposed to are
        within my own knowledge.

2.   I have read what purports to be a copy of the defence delivered by the
        abovenamed Defendants.

3.   In that purported defence the Defendants deny placing any order with my
        company. Now produced and shown marked 'A' is a copy of a letter from
        the Defendants addressed to my company and dated .... ordering
        the goods which are the subject of the Invoices set out in the particulars of
        claim herein.

4.   Prior to the issue of these proceedings written and telephone requests for
        payment were made by the Plaintiffs to the Defendants and at no time did
        the Defendants deny placing an order.

5.   I verily believe that there is no defence to this action, notwithstanding the
        delivery of the purported defence, and I respectfully ask that Judgment be
        entered for the Plaintiffs for the total claim and costs herein pursuant to the
        provisions of Order 9 Rule 14 of the County Court Rules 1981.

Sworn etc.

Figure 8.1 Suggested affidavit – summary judgment

In the _____   County Court

Between: Case No: _____

A. Creditor Limited

Plaintiffs

and

Joseph Debtor

Defendant

This is the Exhibit marked "JS1" referred to in the Affidavit of John Smith sworn the   day of 19

Before me

(Signature of person
administering the Oath)

Figure 8.2 Backsheet to exhibit

The Chief Clerk,
        County Court,

Dear Sir,

Ourselves and Joseph Debtor — Case No.
Pre-Trial Review Date ....

We enclose an original affidavit and two exhibits.

On the hearing of the Pre-Trial Review we intend to apply for summary Judgment.

We have sent copies of the affidavit and exhibits to the Defendant, together with a copy of this letter.

Yours faithfully,

Figure 8.3 Letter advising court of application for summary judgment

IN THE   **COUNTY COURT**

                                                  CASE No.

     Between

                                                                          Plaintiff

                                              AND

                                                                          Defendant

(1) State
nature and
grounds of
application.

I wish to apply for (¹)   . final Judgment in this action pursuant to Order 9 rule 14 of the County Court Rules 1981 on the ground that there is no defence to this action.

     Dated
     (*Signed*)
            Plaintiff/Defendant
     Address for
     service

THIS SECTION TO BE COMPLETED BY THE COURT

To the Plaintiff/Defendant

TAKE NOTICE that this application will be heard by the Registrar [Judge]
at

on   at   o'clock

IF YOU DO NOT ATTEND THE COURT WILL MAKE SUCH ORDER AS IT THINKS FIT.

Address all communications to the Chief Clerk AND QUOTE THE ABOVE CASE NUMBER

THE COURT OFFICE AT

is open from 10 am to 4 pm Monday to Friday.

N.244   Notice of application
       O.13, r.1(2)

oyez   The Solicitors' Law Stationery Society plc, Paulton House, 8 Shepherdess Walk, London N1 7LB   7.89   BM

County Court N244   5039197

Figure 8.4 Notice of applicaton

The Chief Clerk,
        County Court,

Dear Sir,

Ourselves and John Debtor — Case No.

We enclose Notice of Application in triplicate, together with an original affidavit and two exhibits.

Please fix a date for our application for Summary Judgment.

We have sent a copy of this letter, a copy of the affidavit and the exhibits to the Defendant.

                        Yours faithfully,

Figure 8.5 Letter with application for a date for hearing — summary judgment

Chapter 9

Settlements and Arrangements

The issue of a summons may well induce the defendant to contact the plaintiff, to talk. Equally, an unexpected and complex defence, or a defence and counterclaim may suggest to the plaintiff that it would be best to try to settle the matter without going to a hearing.

The parties are perfectly entitled to discuss matters and resolve them. However, the plaintiff should bear in mind that there is a summons before the court which needs to be resolved.

The plaintiff may:

(a) discontinue the action or
(b) accept a lower sum than was claimed, or agree to forego the claim for interest ie compromise in some way or
(c) agree to accept payment by instalments or
(d) agree to pay the *defendant* something (the worst option).

It must be remembered that payments are sent direct to the plaintiff, so the court will not be aware of them. If there are negotiations between the parties to compromise the action, the court will not (nor wish to) know anything about them.

It should be adopted as standard practice that once an action has been commenced in the courts it should be properly concluded — through the courts. The plaintiff should be guided in this by the notes on Form 205A (Figure 4.1). These stipulate the steps the defendant may take on receiving the summons (see Chapter 4). A defendant who simply pays the debt, or part of it, after the issue of the summons, but does nothing else has *not* dealt with the summons. Therefore the plaintiff can tick box A on the request for judgment, complete Section C of that form and obtain judgment for the court fee and interest, or the balance of the debt plus the court fee and interest, on the basis that "The defendant has not replied to my summons".

The plaintiff may decide to exercise one of the options listed in (a) to (d) above. The fact that such an option has been adopted needs to be recorded at the court. That is achieved in various ways, as follows.

The plaintiff discontinues

On being served with the summons the defendant completes Section 3 of Form N9A (Figure 4.5) alleging that the debt was paid before the summons was issued. The court will send a copy of the form to the plaintiff with Form N236 (Figure 9.1).

On checking the records the plaintiff finds that payment was indeed made *before* the summons was issued. He or she therefore ticks the box on Form N236 — "I wish to withdraw the case". The form is signed and returned to the court and the matter is at an end.

The plaintiff may wish to discontinue the action on some other ground. The defence, on investigation, appears to be valid, at least in part. A vital witness may no longer be employed by the plaintiff. Whatever the reason, the plaintiff does not wish to proceed with the action. It is necessary to advise the court of this decision by filing a notice of discontinuance. There is no pre-printed form for this purpose but the draft of a suitable wording is in Figure 9.2.

The document is dated and signed, the original sent to the court and a copy is sent to the defendant. The action is concluded; the plaintiff has indicated that he or she will not continue with it.

Costs

However, the plaintiff must be careful when deciding to take this course of action. If he or she discontinues as a result of a defence other than "claims paid", under the court rules he or she is liable to pay the defendant's costs. If the defendant is dealing with the claim in person he or she cannot claim costs but if solicitors have been instructed and *they* have delivered the defence, costs can be claimed.

If the plaintiff cannot agree a figure for these costs, then the defendant's solicitors are entitled to apply for an order that they be determined by the court. This process will involve further costs which the plaintiff will have to pay. Therefore, starting a speculative action and discontinuing when a defence is filed can prove an expensive exercise.

If the plaintiff wishes to discontinue a defended action when solicitors are involved for the defendant, he or she should attempt to negotiate on the basis that each side bears its own costs. This means that the defendant pays his or her solicitor's costs (see Settlements below).

Counterclaim

If a defence *and* counterclaim is delivered, the plaintiff will be in difficulty if he or she simply discontinues because the counterclaim will remain. The defendant is entitled to proceed with the counterclaim and obtain judgment. Again, if the plaintiff is in this position he or she should attempt to negotiate on the basis that the claim is discontinued and the defendant abandons the counterclaim.

Settlements

Settling an action simply means agreeing some form of compromise to dispose of it without a hearing. Settlements may be on the basis of (b), (c) or (d) above.

The simple way of coming to a settlement is to use the documentation provided by the court. For example, on being served with a summons for £1000 the defendant telephones the plaintiff. He points out that there is a credit note due to him for £100. The plaintiff investigates this and agrees. The easiest way of dealing with that situation is for the plaintiff to agree that if the defendant pays £900 plus the court fee and appropriate interest, the action will be discontinued. The debtor then pays, and the plaintiff files a notice of discontinuance and sends a copy to the defendant. The action is at an end.

However, suppose that having agreed about the £900 plus the court fee and interest, the defendant says that he cannot pay it all at once but wants to discharge it over three months. The plaintiff should tell the defendant to complete the form of admission and offer on that basis and send the completed form to him or her. On receiving it, the plaintiff completes Form N205A accepting the offer. The court will enter judgment for the agreed amount, to be paid as arranged.

If the plaintiff wishes, he or she can accept post-dated cheques for the full amount. However, by adopting this method the plaintiff has secured judgment and, if any cheque is dishonoured, the judgment can be enforced without further delay.

This is preferable to leaving the action simply in mid-air and accepting post-dated cheques. If that course is adopted and a cheque is dishonoured, the plaintiff must apply for judgment, wait for it to be entered and then enforce it.

Instalments

Offers under which the plaintiff agrees to accept something less than the claim, or arrangements for the defendant to pay by instalments, should always be dealt with through the court by using the paperwork served on the defendant with the summons. This is particularly important where the instalment payments are to extend over many months.

Note the wording on the reverse of Form N205A (Figure 4.6):

If (the Plaintiffs) do not ask for Judgment within 12 months of the date of service the action will be struck out. It cannot be reinstated.

Suppose that a summons is served and the defendant contacts the plaintiff and offers to pay by instalments. The debt is £1500 but the defendant can only offer £100 per month.

The plaintiff is satisfied that this is the best offer the debtor can make and the parties agree the total due, including the court fee and interest, and the debtor provides 15 post-dated cheques. The method of "going through the court" is not adopted; thus, it is aware that the summons has been served but, according to its records, nothing further happens.

Suppose that eleven of the defendant's cheques clear but the twelfth one is dishonoured. The plaintiff then applies for judgment for the balance. This is not within 12 months of the date of service, therefore the action has been struck out (dismissed) and cannot be reinstated. The only course now open to the plaintiff is to issue another summons for the balance.

Plaintiffs should adopt a firm policy that all such settlements are dealt with through the court. The court will not enter into correspondence about such settlements but the documents served with the summons can be used as outlined.

Counterclaim

That documentation will not be suitable when there is a counterclaim and some form of compromise is reached. In those circumstances a consent order is the most appropriate method.

For example, the plaintiff claims £3000 plus interest and the court fee. A defence and counterclaim is delivered in which the defendant makes various complaints about the plaintiff's product or service and counterclaims £4000.

After investigation and negotiation it is agreed that the defendant does have some valid complaints justifying a credit of £1000. The plaintiff agrees to accept the sum of £2000 in full and final settlement and the defendant agrees to pay £2000 plus the court fee but not the interest. The plaintiff accepts that arrangement.

There is no way in which the documentation served with the summons can be used by the plaintiff. Indeed, the defendant has used it already, to record his or her defence and counterclaim. The court will not enter into correspondence on this sort of issue, yet the settlement must be formalised, for the protection of both parties.

Form of consent

To do this, the plaintiff prepares a form of consent. There is no prescribed form for this, it is simply typed on plain white A4 paper and it records what has been agreed. An example of a consent is given in Figure 9.3. It is prepared by the plaintiff and signed by plaintiff and defendant. The plaintiff then delivers it to the court with a covering letter: "We enclose a form of consent signed by the parties. Please make an order accordingly".

The court makes the order, the action is concluded on agreed terms and there is no room for disagreement or misunderstanding. Equally, if the defendant does *not* pay as agreed, the plaintiff may proceed to enforcement without further formality or delay.

If the plaintiff found it necessary to pay the defendant something, that too should be recorded (see Figure 9.4).

The terms agreed will be recorded in an order of the court. The provision in Figure 9.4 that "There shall be no Order for costs" means that £400 is all the defendant will be entitled to. He or she will not be able to claim costs because he or she has "won" or because the plaintiff has withdrawn.

The court will make an order on the lines of the consent and send a copy to each party.

Correspondence in negotiations

Chapter 7 dealt with evidence and correspondence. Clearly, there may be correspondence dealing with attempts to negotiate a settlement. The general rule is to mark all such correspondence "without prejudice" so that it cannot be used on a hearing as evidence of the willingness of a party to settle the matter on less favourable terms than his or her claim or counterclaim.

However, the question as to whether a particular letter should be without prejudice or open is one that requires careful consideration. As stated earlier, the general rule is that letters marked without prejudice cannot be produced to the court in the course of the action.

Obviously, if plaintiffs are faced with a substantive counterclaim and wish to discontinue their claim provided the defendant abandons his or her counterclaim, they may well write "without prejudice": "We would be prepared to discontinue our claim provided that you withdraw your counterclaim".

Suppose however that the counterclaim alleges that some goods supplied by the plaintiff were defective. The plaintiff, in negotiations with the defendant, ascertains that only a small amount of the goods are alleged to be defective, but the defendant simply will not pay *anything*. The plaintiff may be prepared to inspect the goods and remedy any agreed defects; the defendant is not prepared to accommodate this. As a sound tactical move the plaintiff may wish to send an open letter along the following lines:

We are perfectly prepared to send our engineer to your premises to inspect the alleged defective goods. If there are defects which can be simply remedied we will have the remedial work done at no cost to you, on the basis that payment is made immediately after the inspection for all goods agreed as satisfactory. This offer remains open for acceptance for seven days from today's date.

The plaintiff is not making any admission as to the alleged defects and may, if the matter proceeds to a hearing, wish the court to see this letter. Thus it is sent as an open letter (ie it is not marked without prejudice). (There is a belief outside the legal profession that all letters in the course of an action should be marked without prejudice. This is not so: there are occasions when a carefully drafted open letter is necessary.)

Settlements and hearing dates

Often negotiations begin in earnest once a date for a hearing is fixed. Indeed, some settlements are concluded just before the parties go into the court for the hearing. The courts do not want to hinder settlements, nor do they want to know how negotiations are progressing. They do, however, need to know as soon as terms are agreed. If, whilst waiting outside the office, of the district judge for an arbitration hearing, the parties reach agreement, the plaintiff may say, on going in for the hearing, "We have agreed terms of settlement in this matter, Sir, and would ask you to make an order that . . . ". The parties will not be criticised for coming to terms, even at this late stage.

However, they will be criticised if they do not advise the court that a settlement has been concluded some time before the hearing date. If a hearing is a few days ahead then the necessary form of consent should be drawn up and signed by the parties. The plaintiff should then telephone the court office to explain that the matter has been settled and that a consent has been signed and is on its way to the court.

If there is sufficient time before the hearing it may not be necessary for anyone to attend. If time is short, the court may advise that the plaintiff should attend, produce the consent and explain to the court that settlement has only recently been arrived at. Plaintiffs must bear in mind the provisions of s.12 of the **Courts and Legal Services Act 1990**. (See Chapter 6 Hearings.)

More actions are settled out of court than are taken to a full hearing since a good "commercial" settlement is preferable to a lengthy and costly trial.

'States Paid' Defence - Plaintiff's Reply

In the	
	County Court
Case No. *Always quote this*	
Defendant	
Plaintiff	
Plaintiff's Ref.	
Court office at	
Telephone	

To the plaintiff

▶ The defendant states that he has paid the amount you are claiming (see enclosed form N9B).

▶ If you disagree and wish to proceed please complete, sign and return this form to the court as soon as possible.

▶ The court will contact you and tell you what to do next.

▶ If the defendant lives in the jurisdiction of another court, the action will be transferred to that court. The court to which the case has been transferred will contact you to tell you what to do next.

▶ If you agree that the defendant has paid, you should complete, sign and return this form to the court withdrawing the case as soon as possible.

To the court

I have read Form N9B and

please tick

☐ I wish to proceed with the case

or

☐ I wish to withdraw the case

Signed _____   Dated _____

To the Chief Clerk

N236 'States paid' defence - plaintiff's reply (Order 9, rules 2 and 5)

Figure 9.1 Form N236

In the   County Court

Between: Case No:

A. Creditor Limited

Plaintiffs

and

Joseph Debtor

Defendant

Notice of Discontinuance

Take Notice that the above named Plaintiffs do not intend to
proceed further in this action and hereby wholly discontinue
the same.

Dated this   day of   19

To the Court
And to the Defendant

Signed: _____
For and on behalf of the
Plaintiffs whose address for
service is

_____

_____

Figure 9.2 Draft notice of discontinuance

In the _____ County Court

Between: Case No: _____

A. Creditor Limited

Plaintiffs

and

Joseph Debtor

Defendant

CONSENT

We, A. Creditor Limited the above named Plaintiff and I Joseph Debtor the above named Defendant **HEREBY CONSENT** to an Order in this action as follows:

1. The Plaintiffs accept the sum of £2,000 in full and final settlement of their claim in this action.

2. The Defendant withdraws the Counterclaim.

3. The Defendant is to pay the above sum of £2,000 by an initial payment of £1,000 to be paid on or before (date). The balance of £1,000 to be paid on or before (date).

Dated the   day of   19

Signed _____   Signed _____
Defendant's name and   For and on behalf of the
address.   Plaintiffs of (address).

Figure 9.3 Draft form of consent

In the   County Court

Between: Case No:

A. Creditor Limited

Plaintiff

and

Joseph Debtor

Defendant

CONSENT

We, A. Creditor Limited the above named Plaintiffs and I Joseph Debtor the above named Defendant **HEREBY CONSENT** to an Order in this action as follows:

1. The Plaintiffs withdraw their claim.

2. The Plaintiffs will pay to the Defendant within 14 days of this Order the sum of £400 which the Defendant will accept in full and final settlement of the Counterclaim.

3. There shall be no Order as to costs.

Dated the   day of   19

Signed _____   Signed _____
Defendant's name and   For and on behalf of the
address.   Plaintiffs of (address).

Figure 9.4 Form of consent − another type

Chapter 10

Enforcing Judgment

Obtaining judgment is one thing, recovering the money due under that judgment is another. The county court offers a range of enforcement processes which can be used in an attempt to compel the defendant to pay. These are:

(a) execution
(b) attachment of earnings
(c) oral examination
(d) garnishee order
(e) charging order
(f) the appointment of a receiver
(g) bankruptcy and liquidation.

It is for the plaintiff to choose which procedure to use and the choice must depend on what is known about the defendant's financial position. Any one of the procedures may be used as soon as judgment is entered.

If one step is taken and proves abortive then the plaintiff may take another course of enforcement action. Obviously, the plaintiff must have regard to the additional fees to be paid for each process and the ultimate prospects of success.

A judgment is no guarantee of payment. The success of any enforcement process depends on the defendant having the money, income or assets to satisfy it.

Execution

This is the method of enforcement most often used. It is a process which empowers the county court bailiff (or in certain cases the sheriff of the county in which the defendant resides or trades) to go to the defendant's premises and demand payment of the judgment debt. If the defendant cannot or will not pay then the bailiff (or sheriff) has power to remove his or her goods, sell them at auction and account to the plaintiff for the proceeds.

The **High Court and County Courts Jurisdiction Order** 1991 has enabled plaintiffs, in certain actions, to instruct the sheriff to enforce a county court judgment instead of the bailiff. The position is:

1. Where the amount to be enforced is £2000 or less it *must* be enforced, under execution, by the county court bailiff.
2. Where the amount is *over* £2000 and up to £5000 it may, as the plaintiff chooses, be enforced by the county court bailiff or by the sheriff.
3. Where the amount is over £5000 it *must* be enforced by the sheriff.

Thus, if the plaintiff wishes to use execution to enforce payment of £1500, he or she must issue a warrant in the county court to be enforced by the bailiff.

If the plaintiff wishes to enforce payment of the sum of £2010, he or she may issue a warrant in the county court or *may* decide to instruct the sheriff.

If he or she wishes to issue execution for a sum of £5000 or more, the sheriff *must* be instructed.

Plaintiffs with a county court judgment for £5000 or more will, however, be able to issue a part warrant where, for example, an instalment due or the final balance is less than £5000.

Bailiff

The bailiff is a full time salaried employee of the county court.

Sheriff

The sheriff is a "freelance" and is paid a commission on what he or she collects as well as fees for his or her efforts. If the sheriff is successful, the fees are five per cent of the first £100 realised and two and half per cent on every £100 thereafter. Often, however, the ongoing interest on the debt will discharge the sheriff's fees. If the sheriff is unsuccessful, the plaintiff will still be charged for the work he or she has done.

Execution in the county court

To issue a warrant in the county court the plaintiff completes Form N323 (Figure 10.1). Section 4 of this form is used to provide the financial details concerning the warrant. At this stage the court will not be aware of any payments made by the defendant since they will have been paid direct to the plaintiff. Thus, the balance that is due at the date of completion of the form must be inserted. They also have to indicate the amount they want to issue the warrant for. A warrant issued for a proportion of the debt is known as a part warrant.

If an order has been made that the defendant should pay by instalments and he or she defaults in payment of an instalment, the plaintiff can:

(a) issue a warrant for all the money due under the judgment or
(b) issue a warrant for *part* of the money due, provided that this is not less than £50 or the amount of one month's instalment.

If the plaintiff decides to issue a part warrant, the amount that will still be owed if the part warrant is paid should be inserted in the space provided on Form N323.

There are two other points of importance in completing the form. First, at the foot of the form there is space for "Other information that might assist the Bailiff". Suppose the plaintiff has a judgment against a limited company and has used the registered office of the company as the address. However, the plaintiff knows that the defendant has premises — a shop or a depot, at another address. If the plaintiff inserts, at the foot of the form, these other addresses then execution will be attempted at all of them.

If the plaintiff has judgment against "Joseph Debtor trading as Owelots" he or she may have sued at the defendant's trading address. That is the address to be entered in box 3. However, the plaintiff can insert Joseph Debtor's home address at the foot of the form. The court will then attempt enforcement at both addresses.

The second significant point about the form is the note "Important. You must inform the Court immediately of any payments you receive after you have sent this request to the Court". Once enforcement action has been put in hand, the plaintiff *must* inform the court, in writing, of any payments received.

The bailiff does not charge any commission on sums recovered. The fee for the issue of the warrant is the only amount payable by the plaintiff. It is added to the debt and is thus recoverable from the defendant.

The fee is inserted in the space provided on the form. The reference to "Land Registry fee" will not apply in cases of trade debt and can be ignored. The "Total" for which the warrant is to be issued is the amount of the warrant, plus the court fee.

The form, plus a cheque for the court fee, is sent to the county court in which the judgment was entered. The court issues a warrant which enables the bailiff to act.

Any money which the bailiff recovers will be paid into the court, which will then account to the plaintiff. If the bailiff is unable to enforce the warrant this will be reported in writing to the plaintiff, giving the reason for non-enforcement (eg "There are no goods of any value on which to levy" or "The defendant has left the given address").

Suspension of the warrant

The visit by the bailiff may lead to the defendant making an application to "suspend" the warrant on the basis that he or she will pay the debt by instalments.

The defendant completes an application, Form N245 (Figure 10.2), and submits it to the court. The court copies it and sends it to the plaintiff with Form N246A (Figure 10.3). If the plaintiff does not reply within 14 days of service on him or her, the court will suspend the warrant on the terms of the offer made using Form N41A (Figure 10.4). A copy will be sent to the plaintiff and to the defendant. If the plaintiff objects to the offer within the 14 days, an officer of the court will decide the issue without a hearing.

As long as the defendant makes the payments ordered, the warrant will remain suspended. If the defendant fails to comply with the order, the plaintiff must apply to re-issue the warrant by completing Form N445 (Figure 10.5) — Request for Re-Issue of Warrant.

The information on this form is identical to that on the request to issue a warrant. However, at the foot of the form the plaintiff completes the section: "Reason for requesting re-issue" (eg "Defendant has failed to comply with the order suspending the warrant dated . . . ").

There is no further fee to pay. The plaintiff simply sends the form to the court and the bailiff will be instructed to enforce the warrant.

The form of request to re-issue can also be used if a warrant has been issued and the bailiff reports that the defendant has left the given address. The debt may be of sufficient value for the plaintiff to make enquiries to trace the defendant. If this trace is successful, the plaintiff completes the request for re-issue of the warrant and gives as the reason for requesting re-issue: "Defendant now resides/ trades at . . . ". There is no further fee to pay and the bailiff will be instructed to levy at the new address.

Plaintiffs should bear in mind that a warrant is valid for 12 months from its issue date. Application can be made to the district judge *before* the date of expiry to extend the period of enforcement. If such an application is made it must be supported by an affidavit explaining why the warrant has not yet been executed and the ground on which an extension is required. Such applications are rare and it is unusual for them to be granted unless there are exceptional circumstances.

Bailiffs do have a heavy workload and plaintiffs should not expect a rapid response to a warrant. Nevertheless, most warrants are dealt with before the time expires.

Exempt goods

Certain goods are exempt, that is protected, from levy. Section 15 of the **Courts and Legal Services Act 1990** stipulates that they are:

(a) such tools, books, vehicles and other items of equipment as are necessary to the defendant for use personally in his or her job or business
(b) such clothing, bedding, furniture, household equipment and provisions as are necessary for satisfying the basic domestic needs of the defendant and his or her family.

These are broad definitions, designed to allow the bailiffs to use their discretion, but the following guidelines have been laid down.

Necessary items

An item should be regarded as necessary if it is so essential that without it there would be no way that the defendant could continue his or her existing job or business.

Motor vehicles

It should be the *exception* rather than the rule that a defendant is allowed to retain a motor vehicle as a necessary item. It is for the defendant to satisfy the bailiff that a vehicle is necessary to allow him or her to continue in his or her job or business.

The fact that a defendant claims to need a vehicle to get to and from a place of work should not, by itself, be considered grounds to exempt the vehicle. The defendant must satisfy the bailiff that no reasonable alternative is available.

Household items

Items such as stereo equipment, televisions and videos, or microwave ovens, where there is also a conventional cooker, are *not* considered to be necessary.

Disputes

If there is a dispute between the bailiff and the defendant in applying these guidelines, the bailiff will refer the matter to the bailiff manager. A levy should be made if at all possible. If the bailiff manager is unable to resolve the dispute he will consult the chief clerk who will decide whether the district judge should be asked to give directions.

Execution via the sheriff

As has been noted, judgments for £2000 or more may, if the plaintiff wishes, be enforced by the sheriff. Judgments of £5000 and over *must* be enforced by the sheriff. The sheriff is instructed by means of a writ of fi.fa. which is issued in the High Court.

First, the plaintiff obtains a certificate of judgment from the county

court in which judgment was entered. The plaintiff then completes
the form of praecipe for the issue of a writ of fi.fa. (Figure 10.6) and
a form of writ of fi.fa. (Figure 10.7). Both these forms are available
from the High Court.

The court fee is paid and the writ of fi.fa. is sealed by the High
Court clerk and handed back to the plaintiff.

The plaintiff posts the sealed copy of the writ to the sheriff of the
county in which the defendant resides or trades, together with a
"lodgement fee" of £2.30. The writ of fi.fa. empowers the sheriff to
levy execution and to report to the plaintiffs.

Note: as can be seen, the issue of a writ of fi.fa. is a High Court
process. The plaintiff is given the right to instruct the sheriff, as
opposed to the bailiff, to expedite execution. However, the Rules of
the High Court specify that a limited company cannot issue *any*
process in the High Court unless it is represented by a solicitor.

Thus, the situation is that an individual who has obtained judgment in the county court and wishes to instruct the sheriff to enforce
it may do so by following the steps above. However, a limited company with a county court judgment must instruct a solicitor to issue
a writ of fi.fa. on its behalf.

Claims by third parties

When the bailiff or sheriff attempts to levy it is necessary to seize
goods which are owned by the defendant. If goods are on hire
purchase, lease or rental they do not belong to the defendant and
thus cannot be taken in execution. Goods may also be claimed by
some third party — the debtor's wife or husband or some other
claimant.

If such a claim is made, the bailiff or sheriff will obtain written
details of the claim and submit it to the plaintiff. The plaintiff must
then admit or reject the claim.

Plaintiffs should consider such claims very carefully, bearing in
mind the amount of the debt and their ability to dispute the claim
of the third party. If the plaintiff accepts the claim made by the third
party, he or she advises the bailiff or sheriff in writing and the
claimed goods cannot then be taken in execution.

If the plaintiff decides to reject the claim this should be advised to
the bailiff or sheriff in writing, and an interpleader summons is then

issued. This brings the plaintiff, the defendant and the claimant before the court to enable the question of ownership of the goods to be determined.

The sheriff or bailiff is the interpleader and takes no sides in the hearing; it is for the plaintiff and the third party to make their case as to ownership. Obviously this can be a difficult task for the plaintiff who may have little evidence as to the rightful ownership of the disputed goods.

If the plaintiff is unable to refute the claim of the third party he or she may have to pay the costs of the hearing. If the claim is refuted, the third party may be ordered to pay the plaintiff's costs or they may be treated as part of the costs of the execution and added to the amount payable by the defendant.

Insolvency — bankruptcy of the defendant

Under the provisions of the **Insolvency Act 1986** the bailiff or sheriff must deliver to a bankrupt's trustee or the liquidator any goods taken in execution or any money realised if they receive notice of the bankruptcy or insolvency of the debtor during the course of the execution.

However, the plaintiff is entitled to money realised under execution, provided the execution is completed before the bankruptcy or insolvency commences. Execution is completed when the defendant's goods have been seized *and* sold.

Where the sum involved exceeds £500 and goods are sold or money paid to avoid a sale, the bailiff or sheriff must retain the money for 14 days. If, during that time, notice of bankruptcy or insolvency is received, the money must be paid over to the bankrupt's trustee or to the insolvency practitioner. It is then part of the assets of the debtor and will be used to pay a dividend to *all* creditors.

Attachment of earnings

This method of enforcement applies only against employees. It cannot be used against the self-employed or against a limited company. It is a process by which the court can make an order against the defendant's employers, ordering them to deduct a specified weekly or monthly sum from his or her wage or salary.

To apply for an attachment order, the plaintiff completes Form N337 (Figure 10.8). He or she should provide as much information as possible about the defendant's employment. If the plaintiff can give detailed information, the court may go direct to the employer if the defendant fails to co-operate. If the plaintiff cannot give sufficient information, the court will require the defendant to complete a questionnaire.

The Form N337 requests the court to deal with the application in the plaintiff's absence (it will not be necessary for the plaintiff to attend on any hearing). The completed form is submitted, with the court fee, to the county court that covers the area in which the defendant resides.

The court will prepare a notice of application for attachment of earnings order, Form N55 (Figure 10.9) and attach to it Form N56 (Figure 10.10). The notice requires the defendant to pay the debt or complete and return Form N56 to the county court within eight days. It also warns the defendant that "Failure to return the reply form and statement of means is a punishable offence. It will result in your employer being contacted and you may also be sent to prison for up to 14 days".

Employer not involved

If the defendant wishes to do so he or she can use Form N56 to make an offer to pay and can apply for leave to pay voluntarily, without the employer being involved. If the defendant does this and if he or she has given sufficient information, the court clerk may make an order. If the defendant has requested it, this may be a suspended order, Form N64 (Figure 10.11). It may be an order against the employer in Form N60 (Figure 10.12).

If the defendant has not given sufficient information to enable the court clerk to make a decision, the papers will be referred to the district judge who may either make an order, or fix a date for the hearing of the application.

Note: if the court clerk makes an order, the plaintiff or the defendant may write to the court objecting to it. In that case a date will be set for the determination of the matter by the district judge.

Failure to return questionnaire

If the defendant fails to return the questionnaire within the time limit, the court will automatically issue an order for production of a statement of means, Form N61A (Figure 10.13).

This is served by the bailiff, on the employer. If the plaintiff has given sufficient information, the court will at the same time serve the employer with a request for a statement of the defendant's earnings.

If the defendant still fails to respond, the court will issue Form N63 (Figure 10.14). This sets a date on which the defendant is required to attend before the district judge to show cause why he or she should not be sent to prison. This is served personally.

Should the defendant still fail to respond, the district judge may issue a warrant committing the defendant to prison, or may order that the defendant be arrested and brought before him or her to give the required information or be sent to prison.

If the court makes a suspended order and the defendant fails to pay, the plaintiff can, by completing Form N446 (Figure 10.15) request the re-issue of the attachment application. No further fee is payable.

As long as an attachment order is in force, the plaintiff may apply at any time, for a variation of the order and the production of an updated statement of the defendant's earnings by completing the application form and paying the fee.

"Attachable" earnings include wages or salary, bonus payments, commissions and overtime pay, and pensions and statutory sick pay.

Pay or allowances to H.M. forces, pensions and benefits under social security provisions and disablement, and disability pensions cannot be attached.

As can be seen this process can take time. However, it will in many cases convince the defendant to pay or to make an offer to pay.

Oral examinations

This is a procedure designed to bring the defendant before the court to be examined, on oath, as to his or her assets, income, liabilities and expenses.

If judgment has been obtained against an individual, that person can be orally examined. If the judgment is against a partnership, a partner may be examined; if it is against a limited company, a named officer of the company can be examined as to the financial position of the company.

The plaintiff completes Form N316 — request for oral examination (Figure 10.16) and submits it, with the court fee, to the county court covering the district in which the defendant resides or trades.

The court will issue an order for oral examination in Form N37 (Figure 10.17) or N38 (Figure 10.18). Note that these orders specify the books and documents which the defendant should produce on the date fixed for the examination. The order will be served on the defendant by post. If he or she or the named officer of the defendant company attends on the hearing, the district judge or the chief clerk will conduct the examination. They will write down the answers given to their questions and require the person being examined to swear on oath that the answers are true. A copy of this document will be sent to the plaintiff.

If the person to be examined fails to attend, the court will adjourn the hearing and issue an order in Form N39 (Figure 10.19). This fixes a further date for the hearing and warns that failure to attend on this occasion may result in imprisonment for contempt to court. N39 is personally served by the bailiff.

In these circumstances the defendant may write to the plaintiff requesting payment of reasonable travel expenses to and from the court. If the plaintiff pays, the sum is added to the debt.

The threat of oral examination or committal may well lead to the defendant making an offer to pay. If the plaintiff wishes to accept the offer, he or she may do so and the hearing of the examination can be adjourned. If it is adjourned and the defendant then defaults in payment, the plaintiff may apply for the hearing to be restored by completing Form N446 (Figure 10.15).

In most cases the chief clerk or district judge will conduct the examination and it will not be necessary for the plaintiff to attend. However, if an N39 is issued, the plaintiff will be given notice and should, at that stage, write to the court asking that the matter be dealt with in his or her absence.

The oral examination may result in the court making an order that the defendant must pay the debt by instalments. It may provide the plaintiff with information as to the assets the defendant has, which may help in deciding on a course of enforcement action by other means (ie execution, charging order, garnishee proceedings).

Garnishee order

Garnishee proceedings are intended to enable a plaintiff who has obtained judgment to obtain payment from any third party that owes the defendant money. A debtor-creditor relationship must exist between the third party and the defendant. Thus, money in the defendant's bank or building society can be "garnisheed"; so can trade debts currently *owed* to the defendant or money held for the defendant by some other person or body.

The plaintiff prepares and swears an affidavit in Form N349 (Figure 10.20). The name and address of the person or body believed to be indebted to the debtor is inserted in paragraph 3. The words in the square brackets in this paragraph may, if the plaintiff cannot specify the exact sum due, be amended to read "in a sum sufficient to satisfy the judgment debt". The plaintiff must also state the ground of his or her information and belief. For example, if he or she is going against the defendant's bank, he or she may say: "When applying to open the credit account with the plaintiff the defendant stated he banked with XY Bank Limited and since then certain payments have been made to the plaintiff by cheques drawn on that bank".

If the plaintiff is seeking to go against a person or business thought to owe the defendant money, he or she may say: "In a telephone conversation on 15th May the defendant stated that XY & Co. owed him £10,000 which he expected to be paid by the end of the month".

If the plaintiff is seeking to garnishee the defendant's bank or building society account, it is necessary to give details of the branch at which the defendant's account is maintained and, if possible, the account number in paragraph 4.

The affidavit is sworn and lodged with the county court in which the judgment was obtained, with the appropriate fee. The court will then draw up a garnishee order to show cause, also known as a Garnishee Order Nisi — Form N84 (Figure 10.21). This order will be served on the third party and a copy will be served on the defendant. As from the date of service of the order the money held by the third party is "frozen" and may not be paid to any party until the court has made a final order.

If the third party admits to holding sufficient money to satisfy the judgment, the court will, on the date fixed for hearing, make the order "absolute" (final). The order will be Form N85 (Figure 10.22) and it directs the third party to pay the amount of the debt to the plaintiff.

If the third party is a bank or building society, then the third party may, at any time before the hearing, give written notice to the court that it does not hold any money for the credit of the defendant. In that event the claim will not proceed.

Timing

The garnishee process will only be effective if money is due to the defendant at the date of service of the order. Thus, timing is crucial: money which is due *after* the date of service is not caught by the order. If the order is served on the defendant's bank and, at the date of service, no cleared funds are available, the garnishee process will fail.

Other methods of enforcement are available and are considered in Chapter 11.

Request for Warrant of Execution

(to be completed and signed by the Plaintiff or his Solicitor and sent to the court with the appropriate fee)

1 Plaintiff's
Name and
Address.

In the

County Court

Case Number

2 Name and
Address for
Service and
Payment
(if different
from above).

Ref/Tel No.

for court use only

Warrant no.

Issue date:

Warrant applied for at   o'clock

3 Defendant's
Name and
Address.

Foreign court code/name:

I certify that the whole or part of any
instalments due under the judgment or
order have not been paid and the balance
now due is as shown

4 Warrant details

(A) Balance due at date of this request

(B) Amount for which warrant to issue

Issue fee

Solicitor's costs

Land Registry fee

TOTAL

If the amount of the warrant at (B) is
less than the balance at (A), the sum
due after the warrant is paid will be

Signed

Plaintiff (Plaintiff's solicitor)

Dated

**IMPORTANT
You must inform the court
immediately of any payments
you receive after you have sent
this request to the court**

*Other information that might assist the bailiff including the name(s) and address(es) of any 2nd/3rd Defendant and other
address(es) at which the Defendant might have goods. You should also tell the court if you have reason to believe that the
bailiff might encounter serious difficulties in attempting to execute the warrant.*

Warrant No.

N323 Request for warrant of execution (Order 26, rule 1(1))

OYEZ The Solicitors' Law Stationery Society Ltd, Oyez House, 7 Spa Road, London SE16 3QQ   1990 Edition   7.91 F20286
                                                                                                                      5039341
County Court N323

Figure 10.1 Request for warrant of execution

Application for suspension of a warrant and/or variation of an order	In the

Application for suspension of a warrant and/or variation of an order

- Read these notes carefully before completing the form.
- Tick the correct boxes and give as much information as you can. It will help the court make a fair decision about how much you can afford to pay if the plaintiff refuses your offer.
- If you do not complete all the details and sign the form, the court will not be able to deal with your application.
- The court will send you an order giving details of how and when to pay or will tell you when to come to court. You will be informed of the court's decision.

In the

LEEDS County Court

Case Number	Always quote this	
Warrant No		**Local No**

Plaintiff (including ref.)

Defendant

For court use only	Date copy sent to plaintiff	

I cannot pay the amount ordered and

I wish to apply for

☐ suspension of the warrant and/or

☐ a reduction in the instalment order

1 Personal details

Surname

Forename

☐ Mr ☐ Mrs ☐ Miss ☐ Ms

☐ Married ☐ Single ☐ Other (specify)

Age

Address

2 Dependants (people you look after financially)

Number of children in each age group

under 11 ☐ 11-15 ☐ 16-17 ☐ 18 & over ☐

Other dependants (give details)

3 Employment

☐ I am employed as a

My employer is

Jobs other than main job (give details)

☐ I am self employed as a

Annual turnover is . . . . £

☐ I am not in arrears with my national insurance contributions, income tax and VAT

☐ I am in arrears and I owe . . . . £

Give details of:
(a) contracts and other work in hand
(b) any sums due for work done

☐ I have been unemployed for ____ years ____ months

☐ I am a pensioner

4 Bank account and savings

☐ I have a bank account

☐ The account is in credit by . . . . . £

☐ The account is overdrawn by . . . £

☐ I have a savings account or building society account

The amount in the account is . . . £

5 Property

I live in ☐ my own property ☐ lodgings

☐ jointly owned property ☐ council property

☐ rented property

N245 Form for applying for suspension of warrant of execution or reduction of instalment order (Order 13, rule 1(2), Order 22, rule 10(4), Order 25, rule 8) MCR 2649/SP 91 7/91

Figure 10.2 Application to suspend warrant

6 Income

My usual take home pay *(including overtime, commission, bonuses etc)*	£	per
Income support	£	per
Child benefit(s)	£	per
Other state benefit(s)	£	per
My pension(s)	£	per
Others living in my home give me	£	per
Other income *(give details below)*		
	£	per
	£	per
	£	per
Total income	£	per

8 Priority debts

(This section is for arrears only. Do not include regular expenses listed in box 7)

Rent arrears	£	per
Mortgage arrears	£	per
Community charge arrears	£	per
Water charges arrears	£	per
Fuel debts: Gas	£	per
Electricity	£	per
Other	£	per
Maintenance arrears	£	per
Others *(give details below)*		
	£	per
	£	per
Total priority debts	£	per

7 Expenses

(Do not include any payments made by other members of the household out of their own income)

I have regular expenses as follows:

Mortgage *(including second mortgage)*	£	per
Rent	£	per
Community charge	£	per
Gas	£	per
Electricity	£	per
Water charges	£	per
TV rental and licence	£	per
HP repayments	£	per
Mail order	£	per
Housekeeping, food, school meals	£	per
Travelling expenses	£	per
Children's clothing	£	per
Maintenance payments	£	per
Others *(not court orders or credit debts listed in boxes 9 and 10)*		
	£	per
	£	per
	£	per
Total expenses	£	per

9 Court orders

Court	Case No.	£	per

Total court order instalments	£	**per**

Of the payments above, I am behind with payments to *(please list)*

10 Credit debts

Loans and credit card debts *(please list)*

	£	per
	£	per
	£	per

Of the payments above, I am behind with payments to *(please list)*

11 Offer of Payment

• *If you take away the totals of boxes 7, 8 and 9 and the payments you are making in box 10 from the total in box 6, you will get some idea of the sort of sum you should offer. The offer you make should be one you can afford.*

I can pay £   a month

(and I enclose £   )

12 Declaration

I declare that the details I have given above are true to the best of my knowledge

Signed   Dated

N245

Figure 10.2 (continued)

Plaintiff's Reply to Defendant's Application to Suspend Warrant

To the plaintiff ('s solicitor)

In the	
	County Court
Case Number *Always quote this*	
Warrant No.	**Local No.**
Plaintiff	
Defendant	
Plaintiff's Ref.	

Enclosed is a copy of an application made by the defendant for suspension of the warrant issued in this case (and/or for a variation of the order made.)

- The court will make an order in the terms of the defendant's offer unless you write to the court with your objections. You have 16 days from the date of the postmark to do this.
- Only **one** box should be ticked.
- Please remember to sign and date the form.

If you ACCEPT the defendant's offer

1. ☐ **I accept the defendant's offer**
   - Return the form to the court office within the 16 day time limit (explained above).
   - The court will make an order suspending the warrant (and varying the order) so long as payment is made in accordance with the offer.

Note If the defendant does not keep up the payments, you may ask the court to reissue the warrant. Ask at the court office for Form N445.

If you AGREE to the suspension but DO NOT ACCEPT the defendant's offer (eg because you think the defendant could pay more)

2. ☐ **I do not accept the defendant's offer of payment but I will accept payment**
   (by instalments of £   per month) or (in full by   199   )
   - Give your reasons in the space below.
   - Return the form to the court office within the 16 day time limit (explained above).
   - The court will fix the rate of payment and will send you and the defendant a copy of the order.

If you DO NOT AGREE to the suspension and you DO NOT ACCEPT the defendant's offer

3. ☐ **I do not accept the defendant's offer of payment because I wish the bailiff to proceed with the warrant**
   - Give your reasons in the space below.
   - Return the form to the court office within the 16 day time limit (explained above).
   - The court will return a copy of this form to you showing the date when the application and your objections will be heard. (The defendant will also receive a copy.)
   - If you do not attend the hearing, the court will make an order in your absence.

Record here your objections to the defendant's proposals *(continue on a separate sheet if necessary)*

Signed .... Plaintiff ('s solicitor)   **Dated** ....

⌐ **This section to be completed by the court**

To the plaintiff and defendant

Date hearing notice sent

Take Notice that the defendant's application will be heard by the court
at
on   at   o'clock

If you do not attend the hearing the court will make an order in your absence

The court office at

is open between 10 am and 4 pm Monday to Friday. When corresponding with the court, please address forms or letters to the Chief Clerk and quote the case number.
N246A Plaintiff's reply to defendant's application to suspend warrant of execution (Order 13, rule 1(2), Order 25, rule 8)   Dd 8252132 100M 5/91 Ed(289333)

Figure 10.3 Form N246A

Order Suspending Warrant

Plaintiff   (determination)

Defendant

In the	County Court
Case No. *Always quote this*	
Warrant No.	
Local No.	
Plaintiff's Ref.	

Seal

On the application of the defendant

And the court having considered the papers received from the parties and being satisfied that the defendant is unable to pay and discharge the sum payable by him in this action (or the instalments due under the judgment or order in this action)

It is ordered that

This warrant of execution and the judgment (or order) be suspended and not enforced so long as the defendant do pay the plaintiff the outstanding sum of £   (by instalments of £   for every calendar month, the first payment to reach the plaintiff)

<u>by</u>   and further payments to reach the plaintiff

by the   day of each month

* delete as necessary

(The warrant will be returned to the   County Court after 16 days. After that date any further correspondence should be sent there, quoting the court case number)*

Dated

———— **Take Notice** ————

If you (either the plaintiff or defendant) object to the payment rate fixed by the court, you must write to the court with your reasons. You have 16 days from the date of the postmark to do this. A hearing will be arranged and both parties will be told when to come to court.

———— **Address for Payment** ————

To the defendant

If you do not pay in accordance with this order the warrant may be reissued or other enforcement proceedings may be taken against you. If your circumstances change and you cannot pay, ask at the court office about what you can do.

———— **How to Pay** ————

- PAYMENT(S) MUST BE MADE to the person named at the address for payment quoting their reference and the court case number.
- DO NOT bring or send payments to the court. THEY WILL NOT BE ACCEPTED.
- You should allow <u>at least</u> 4 days for your payment to reach the plaintiff or his representative.
- Make sure that you keep records and can account for all payments made. Proof may be required if there is any disagreement. It is not safe to send cash unless you use registered post.
- A leaflet giving further advice about payment can be obtained from the court.
- If you need more information you should contact the plaintiff or his representative.

The court office at

is open between 10 am and 4 pm Monday to Friday. When corresponding with the court, please address forms or letters to the Chief Clerk and quote the case number

N41A Order suspending warrant (determination) (Order 25,rule 8)

Figure 10.4 Order suspending warrant

Request for Reissue of Warrant

(tick appropriate box and enter case number and warrant number)

	In the
	County Court
	Case Number
	Warrant Number

Type of warrant

- [ ] **Warrant of execution**
- [ ] **Warrant of possession**
- [ ] **Warrant of delivery**
- [ ] **Warrant of committal**

For court use only

Wt. Reissue No.

Reissue date:

Foreign court code/name:

1 Plaintiff's Name.

2 Name and Address for Service and Payment.

Ref./Tel. No.

3 Defendant's Name and Address.

I certify that the whole or part of any instalments due under the judgment or order have not been paid and the balance now due is as shown (* and that the amount due under the part warrant is as shown at (B))

4 Warrant details

(A) Balance of judgment or order due at date of this request (including fee and costs of warrant issue where warrant reissued for full amount or balance)

Signed

Plaintiff (Plaintiff's solicitor)

(B) Part warrants only
Balance due under the warrant (including the fee and costs of warrant issue)

Dated

(*delete if not a part warrant)

If the amount of the warrant at (B) is less than the balance at (A), the sum due after the warrant is paid will be

IMPORTANT
You must inform the court immediately of any payments you receive after you have sent this request to the court

Reasons for requesting reissue (information you are relying on to support your application for reissue eg address for execution has changed, failure to make payments under a suspended order etc. You should also tell the court if you have reason to believe that the bailiff might encounter any serious difficulty in attempting to execute the warrant.)

Reissue No.

N445 Request for reissue of warrant (Order 26, rule 8(5)(b))

oyez The Solicitors' Law Stationery Society Ltd., Oyez House, 27 Crimscott Street, London SE1 5TS

2.90 F16186

5039618

County Court N445

Figure 10.5 Request to re-issue warrant

Praecipe for
Writ of Fieri Facias
(District Registry)
(O.46, r.6)

IN THE HIGH COURT OF JUSTICE
Division

19   .—   .—High Court No.
County Court Plaint No.

[(On transfer from the   County Court)]

Between

Plaintiff

AND

Defendant

Seal a Writ of Fieri Facias directed to the sheriff of

against

of

in the County of

(1) Or "Order" or "Award".

upon a Judgment (¹)   [of the   County Court]

dated the   day of   , 19   , for the sum

of £   debt and £   costs and interest, etc.

(2) Insert the appropriate rate of interest at date of entry of judgment.

Indorsed to levy £   and interest thereon at (²)   per

cent per annum, from the   day of   19   ,

and £   costs of execution

(Solicitors name)
(Address)

Agent for

of

Solicitor   for the

Dated this   day of   19

Figure 10.6 Praecipe for writ of fi. fa.

19   .—   .—No.

IN THE HIGH COURT OF JUSTICE
Division
District Registry

PRAECIPE
For Writ of Fieri Facias

Solicitor

Solicitor's Reference

oyez The Solicitors' Law Stationery Society plc, Oyez House,
27 Crimscott Street, London SE1 5TS   7 86 F6329
5050026
High Court E1*   • • • •

Figure 10.6 (reverse)

Writ of
Fieri Facias
(O. 45, r. 12)

IN THE HIGH COURT OF JUSTICE 19   .—   .—High Court No.
                    Division   **County Court Plaint No.**
                 District Registry

[Transferred from the   County Court
by certificate dated the   day of   19   ]
Between

                                                                    Plaintiff

AND

                                                                    Defendant

ELIZABETH THE SECOND, by the Grace of God, of the United Kingdom of Great
Britain, Northern Ireland and of Our other realms and territories Queen, Head of
the Commonwealth, Defender of the Faith.
To the sheriff of   greeting:
Whereas in the above-named action it was on the   day of

(1) "adjudged"   , 19   , (1)   in this Court [or in the
or "ordered".   County Court under Plaint No.   ]

(2) Name   that the Defendant (2)
of Defendant.

(3) Name   do   pay the Plaintiff (3)
of Plaintiff.   £   [and £   [costs] [costs to be taxed, which
                    costs have been taxed and allowed at £   as appears by the
                    certificate of the District Registrar at
                    dated the   day of   , 19   .]]:
                    WE COMMAND YOU that of the goods, chattels and other property of (2)

                    in your county authorised by law to be seized in execution you cause to be made the
(4) The words in   sum[s] of £   (4) [and £   for costs of
this set of square
brackets are to be execution] and also interest on £   at the rate of £   (5)
omitted where the
judgment or order   per cent per annum from the   day of   , 19   , until
is for less than
£600 and does not   payment(4) [together with sheriff's poundage, officers' fees, costs of levying and all
entitle the Plaintiff
to costs against the other legal, incidental expenses] and that immediately after execution of this writ you
person   against
whom the writ is   pay (3)
issued.   In pursuance of the said (6)   the amount levied in respect of the
(5) Insert   the said sums and interest.
appropriate rate of
interest at the date AND WE ALSO COMMAND YOU that you indorse on this writ immediately after
of entry of judg-
ment.   execution thereof a statement of the manner in which you have executed it and send
(6) "judgment" or   a copy of the statement to (3)
"order".
                    Witness

                                                  Lord High Chancellor of Great Britain,
                    the   day of   , 19   .

Figure 10.7 Writ of fi. fa.

This Writ was issued by
of

[Agent for
of

Solicitor for the Plaintiff who reside at

The Defendant resides at

in the County of

High Court F1* (DR)

Figure 10.7 (reverse)

Request for Attachment of Earnings Order

(to be completed and signed by the Plaintiff or his Solicitor and sent to the court with the appropriate fee)

1 Plaintiff's Name and Address

In the

County Court

Case Number

2 Name and Address for Service and Payment (if different from above) Ref./Tel. No.

For court use only

A/E application no.

Issue date:

Hearing date:

on

at   o'clock

at (address)

3 Defendant's Name and Address

4 Judgment details
Court where judgment/order made if not court of issue

I apply for an attachment of earnings order

I certify that the whole or part of any instalments due under the judgment or order have not been paid and the balance now due is as shown.

5 Outstanding debt
Balance due at date of this request* (excluding issue fee but including unsatisfied warrant costs)

Issue fee

AMOUNT NOW DUE

*You may also be entitled to interest to date of request where judgment is for over £5,000 and is entered on or after 1 July 1991

Signed

Plaintiff (Plaintiff's solicitor)

Dated

6 Employment Details (please give as much information as you can — it will help the court to make an order more quickly)

Employer's name and address

7 Other Details (Give any other details about the Defendant's circumstances which may be relevant to the application)

Defendant's place of work (if different from employer's address)

The Defendant is employed as

Works No./Pay Ref.

IMPORTANT
You must inform the court immediately of any payments you receive after you have sent this request to the court.

N337   Request for attachment of earnings order (Order 27, rule 4(1))

OYEZ The Solicitors' Law Stationery Society Ltd, Oyez House, 7 Spa Road, London SE16 3QG

1991 Edition 5.91 F19960
5039383

County Court N337

Figure 10.8 Attachment of earnings application

Notice of Application for Attachment of Earnings Order

Plaintiff

In the _____ **County Court**

Defendant

Case No.	*Always quote this*	
Application No.		
Plaintiff's Ref.		

To the defendant

(Seal)

The plaintiff obtained a judgment (or order) against you in this court

(1) or as the case may be (_____)(1)

And as you have failed to pay as ordered, the plaintiff has applied for an attachment of earnings order requiring your employer to make deductions from your earnings to pay the judgment (or order)

Unless you pay the plaintiff the amount now due (shown below), you must complete the enclosed form of reply, including the statement of means, and send it to reach the court office **within 8 days** after you receive this notice

Failure to return the reply form and statement of means is a punishable offence. It will result in your employer being contacted and you may also be sent to prison for up to 14 days.

(2) where judgment entered for more than £5,000 on or after 1 July 1991

Balance of debt due at date of this notice (and any interest (2))	£	
Attachment issue fee	£	
AMOUNT NOW DUE	£	

Dated

Instructions - please read these carefully

- If the plaintiff's claim includes interest(2) and you pay the amount now due within 8 days after you receive this notice, the plaintiff will not be entitled to further interest. If you wish to pay the amount due, see **How to Pay** below.
- If you complete and return the form of reply, including the statement of means, within 8 days and the court is satisfied with the information you give, the court will make an order and send you a copy. You will not have to attend court.
- If you are unemployed or self employed, you should say so on the form of reply and answer as many questions as you can.

- If you want an opportunity to pay voluntarily without your employer being ordered to make deductions from your pay, you should ask for a suspended order on the form of reply. You should also enclose a copy of your most recent pay slip.
- Read the notes on the form of reply before giving the details asked for.
- You can obtain help in completing the enclosed form of reply at any county court office or citizens' advice bureau

── Address for Payment ──

── How to Pay ──

- PAYMENT(S) MUST BE MADE to the person named at the address for payment quoting their reference and the court case number.
- DO NOT bring or send payments to the court. THEY WILL NOT BE ACCEPTED.
- You should allow <u>at least</u> 4 days for your payment to reach the plaintiff or his representative.
- Make sure that you keep records and can account for all payments made. Proof may be required if there is any disagreement. It is not safe to send cash unless you use registered post.
- A leaflet giving further advice about payment can be obtained from the court.
- If you need more information you should contact the plaintiff or his representative.

The court office at

is open between 10 am and 4 pm Monday to Friday. When corresponding with the court, please address forms or letters to the Chief Clerk and quote the case number

N55 Notice of application for attachment of earnings order (Order 27, rule 5(1))

Figure 10.9 Notice of application for attachment

Case No _____

Warrant
Number _____

Date of order _____

APPLICANT

Applicant (solicitor)'s address

Warrant for Possession of Land under Order 24

To the district judge and bailiffs of the court

On the   day of   19

(1) describe the land set out in the order

It **was ordered** that the applicant recover possession of [1].

Ref. _____

RESPONDENT(S)

(**And it was ordered** that the applicant do recover against the respondent the sum of £   for costs, making together the sum of £   , which the respondent was ordered to pay to the applicant **by**   )

Address(es) to levy at

THE RESPONDENT HAS FAILED TO OBEY THE ORDER AND AT THE APPLICANT'S REQUEST THIS WARRANT HAS BEEN ISSUED. YOU ARE NOW REQUIRED TO GIVE POSSESSION OF THE LAND TO THE APPLICANT.

(**You are further required** to levy for the total shown overleaf, in accordance with the provisions of sections 85 and 89 of the County Courts Act 1984.)

Application was made to this court for this warrant at   minutes past the hour

of   o'clock on

Balance of debt	
Amount of warrant Fee	
Solicitor's costs	
Land Registry fee	
Total	

The bailiff should give a printed and numbered receipt from his official receipt book for every payment made to him under this warrant. You should not accept any other form of receipt.

For more information see over

N52 Warrant for possession of land under Order 24 (Order 24, rule 6(1))

Figure 10.9 (continued)

<table>
<tr><td colspan="2">

Form for Replying to an Attachment of Earnings Application

</td><td colspan="2">

In the _____   County Court

Case Number _Always quote this_

Application Number

Plaintiff _(including ref.)_

Defendant

</td></tr>
</table>

- Read the notes on the notice of application before completing this form.

- Tick the correct boxes and give as much information as you can. The court will make an order based on the information you give on this form. You must give full details of your employment and your income and outgoings. Enclose a copy of your most recent pay slip if you can.

- _Make your offer of payment in box 10. You will get some idea of how much to offer by adding up your expenses in boxes 6, 7, 8 and 9 and taking them from your total income (box 5)._

- Send or take this completed and signed form immediately to the court office shown on the notice of application.

- You should keep your copy of the notice of application unless you are making full payment. (This does not apply to maintenance applications.)

- For details of where and how to pay see notice of application.

1 Personal details

Surname

Forename

☐ Mr   ☐ Mrs   ☐ Miss   ☐ Ms
☐ Married   ☐ Single   ☐ Other _(specify)_

Age

Address

Postcode

2 Dependants _(people you look after financially)_

Number of children in each age group

under 11 ☐   11-15 ☐   16-17 ☐   18 & over ☐

Other dependants _(give details)_

3 Employment

I am   ☐ employed as a _____
         ☐ self employed as a _____
         ☐ unemployed
         ☐ a pensioner

a. employment

My employer is

Employer's address

Address of employer's head office _(if different from above)_

My works number and / or pay reference is

Jobs other than main job _(give details)_

b. self employment

Length of time self employed   years   months

c. unemployment
Length of time unemployed   years   months

Give details of any outstanding interviews

4 Bank account and savings

☐ I have a bank account
   ☐ The account is in credit by ..... £
   ☐ The account is overdrawn by .. £

☐ I have a savings or building society account
   The amount in the account is ... £

N56 Statement of means - attachment of earnings (Order 27, rule 5(1))

Figure 10.10 Statement of means

For court use only

Certificate of Service - Attachment of Earnings	Case No

I certify that the notice of which this is a true copy, together with a form of reply was

served by me on (date) ....

Service was effected *(tick and complete whichever applies)*

☐   by posting it to the defendant on   at the address stated in the notice.

☐   by delivering it to the defendant personally (or to   )

       apparently not less than 16 years old, who promised to give it to the defendant on the same day)
       (or on   )

       at the address stated in the notice (or at   )

☐   by inserting it, enclosed in an envelope addressed to the defendant, in the letter box at the address
       stated on the notice. I have reason to believe that the notice will reach the defendant in sufficient
       time, because:

                                                      Bailiff / Officer of the Court

OR

I certify that the notice has not been served for the following reasons:

                                                      Bailiff / Officer of the Court

Figure 10.10 (continued)

Suspended Attachment of Earnings Order

Plaintiff	In the	County Court

Case No.	*Always quote this*	
A/E No.		
Plaintiff's Ref.		

Defendant

Seal

It is ordered that the attachment of earnings order made in this case
be suspended and not enforced so long as the defendant punctually pays the
plaintiff the sum of £   by instalments of £   for
every calendar month (week), the first instalment to reach the plaintiff
by   until £   , the amount

* where judgment is for more than £5000 and was entered on or after 1 July 1991

payable under the order, together with any interest,* has been paid

It is further ordered that service of the order on the employer be deferred
accordingly

Dated

** If you (either the plaintiff or the defendant) object to the terms contained in this order, you must write to the court with your reasons.
y ou have 16 days from the date of the postmark to do this. A hearing will be arranged and both parties will be told when to come to court.*

* Delete where order made by district judge at hearing

———— Take Notice ————

To the defendant

At your request the court has made a suspended attachment of earnings order. This means that your employer will not be told that an order has been made against you so long as you keep your payments up to date. If you fall behind with your payments, the plaintiff may ask the court to send the order to your employer for payments to be deducted from your earnings without further notice.

If you change your employer, you must notify the court in writing within 7 days giving the following details

- the name and address of your new employer (and the pay office if different)
- your works number and / or pay reference
- your new rate of pay
- the court case number

IF YOU DO NOT DO WHAT THIS NOTICE TELLS YOU, YOU MAY BE FINED OR IMPRISONED OR BOTH

———— Address for Payment ————

———— How to Pay ————

- **PAYMENT(S) MUST BE MADE** to the person named at the address for payment quoting their reference and the court case number.
- **DO NOT bring or send payments to the court. THEY WILL NOT BE ACCEPTED.**
- You should allow <u>at least</u> 4 days for your payment to reach the plaintiff or his representative.
- Make sure that you keep records and can account for all payments made. Proof may be required if there is any disagreement. It is not safe to send cash unless you use registered post.
- A leaflet giving further advice about payment can be obtained from the court.
- If you need more information you should contact the plaintiff or his representative.

The court office at

is open between 10 am and 4 pm Monday to Friday. When corresponding with the court, please address forms or letters to the Chief Clerk and quote the case number.

N64 Suspended attachment of earnings order (Order 27, rule 10)

Figure 10.11 Suspended attachment order

Certificate of Service (to be completed by the court)

I certify that the order of which this is a true copy was served by me on the defendant personally at the address stated in the order, or at

on the   day of   19

Bailiff / Officer of the Court
Date

I certify that the order has **not been served** for the following reason:

Bailiff / Officer of the Court
Date

Figure 10.11 (reverse)

Attachment of Earnings Order

To the defendant's employer

In the	
	County Court
Case No. *Always quote this*	
Application No.	
Plaintiff	
Defendant	
Plaintiff's Ref.	

Seal

The defendant who is employed by you at

as a (works no/pay ref)
(1) or as the case may be
is in arrears under a judgment of this court ( ) (1)
and earnings are payable by you to the defendant

You are therefore ordered to make periodical deductions out of the defendant's earnings in accordance with the Attachment of Earnings Act 1971 until £ , the amount payable under the judgment has been paid

For the purpose of calculating the deductions
- The normal deduction rate is £ per week / month
- The protected earnings rate is £ per week / month

And you are ordered to pay the sums deducted into the office of this court at monthly intervals

Dated

*If you (either the plaintiff or defendant) object to the terms for payment contained in this order, you must write to the court with your reasons. You have 16 days from the date of the postmark to do this. A hearing will be arranged and you will both be told when to come to court

*delete where order made by district judge at hearing

——— **Take Notice** ———

To the defendant

This is a copy of an attachment of earnings order sent to your employer

If you change your employer, you must notify the court in writing within 7 days, giving the following details:

- the name and address of your new employer (and the pay office if different)
- your works number and / or pay reference

- your new rate of pay
- the court case number

If you do not do what this notice tells you, you may be fined or imprisoned or both

Defendant's address

When corresponding with the court, please address forms or letters to the Chief Clerk and quote the case number.
The court office at

is open between 10 am and 4 pm Monday to Friday

N60 Attachment of earnings order (judgment debt) (Order 27, rule 10)

Figure 10.12 Order against employer

Certificate of Service (to be completed by the court)

I certify that the order of which this is a true copy was served by me on the defendant personally at the address stated in the order, or at

on the   day of   19

Bailiff / Officer of the Court

Date

I certify that the order has **not been served** for the following reason:

Bailiff / Officer of the Court

Date

Figure 10.12 (reverse)

Order to Produce a
Statement of Earnings

To the defendant's employer

In the	
	County Court
Case No. *Always quote this*	
Application No.	
Plaintiff	
Defendant	

Seal

For the purposes of an application for an attachment of earnings order in respect of the above named defendant

You are ordered to complete the enclosed statement of earnings and send it to reach the court office **within 8 days** after service of this order upon you

Dated

———— **Take Notice** ————

Failure to return the completed statement of earnings form may result in a fine of up to £100 under Section 23 of the Attachment of Earnings Act 1971

The court office at

is open between 10 am and 4 pm Monday to Friday
When corresponding with the court, please address forms or letters to the Chief Clerk and quote the case number

N61A Order to employer for production of statement of earnings (Order 27, rule 15(1))
•

Figure 10.13 Order for statement of means

For court use only

Certificate of Service - Attachment of Earnings	Case No

I certify that the notice of which this is a true copy, together with a form of reply was

served by me on (date) ....

Service was effected *(tick and complete whichever applies)*

☐   by posting it to the defendant on   at the address stated in the notice.

☐   by delivering it to the defendant personally (or to   )

apparently not less than 16 years old, who promised to give it to the defendant on the same day)
(or on   )

at the address stated in the notice (or at   )

☐   by inserting it, enclosed in an envelope addressed to the defendant, in the letter box at the address stated on the notice. I have reason to believe that the notice will reach the defendant in sufficient time, because:

Bailiff / Officer of the Court

OR

I certify that the notice has not been served for the following reasons:

Bailiff / Officer of the Court

Figure 10.13 (reverse)

Failure to Provide
Statement of Means

To the defendant

In the	
	County Court
Case No. *Always quote this*	
Application No.	
Plaintiff	
Defendant	
Plaintiff's Ref.	

Seal

You have failed to give the court within the time specified a statement of your earnings, resources and means in accordance with section 14 of the Attachment of Earnings Act 1971

You are therefore ordered to attend court in person

at

on the   at   o'clock

(1) delete as appropriate

to give good reasons (why you should not be arrested and brought before this court when you may be sent to prison for up to 14 days (1) **) (or fined up to £100 under Section 23 of the Attachment of Earnings Act 1971** (1) **)**

Dated

(2) see * below

If you **immediately return** the completed and signed form of reply and statement of means to the court or pay into the court office (£   (2) the sum remaining due, you may not have to attend

Instructions - please read these carefully

- *If you wish to pay the amount see **Payments into Court**. Where judgment was entered on or after 1 July 1991, this amount may include interest. If so, the plaintiff may claim further interest until final payment.
- If you complete and return the form of reply, including the statement of means, within 8 days and the court is satisfied with the information you give, it will send you a copy of the order.
- If you are unemployed or self employed, you should say so on the form of reply and answer as many questions as you can.
- If you want an opportunity to pay voluntarily without your employer being ordered to make deductions from your pay, you should ask for a suspended order on the form of reply. You should also include a copy of your most recent pay slip.
- Read the notes on the form of reply before giving the details asked for.
- You can obtain help in completing the enclosed form of reply at any county court office or citizens' advice bureau.

The court office at

is open between 10 am and 4 pm Monday to Friday. When corresponding with the court, please address forms or letters to the Chief Clerk and quote the case number.

————— Payments into Court —————
please bring or enclose this form

You can pay the court by calling at the court office which is open from 10 am to 4 pm Monday to Friday.

You may only pay by:
- cash
- banker's or giro draft
- cheque supported by a cheque card
- cheque (unsupported cheques may be accepted, subject to clearance, if the Chief Clerk agrees)

Cheques / drafts must be made out to HM Paymaster General and crossed.

By post
You may only pay by:
- postal order
- banker's or giro draft
- cheque (cheques may be accepted, subject to clearance, if the Chief Clerk agrees)

The payment must be made out to HM Paymaster General and crossed. This method of payment is at your own risk.
And you must:
- pay the postage
- enclose a self addressed envelope so that the court can return the form and a receipt

The court cannot accept stamps or payments by bank and giro credit transfers.

Note: You should carefully check any future forms from the court to see if payments should be made directly to the plaintiff.

N63 Notice to show cause under Section 23 of the Attachment of Earnings Act 1971 (Order 27, rule 7A(2))

Figure 10.14 Order to show cause

Certificate of Service (to be completed by the court)

I certify that the order of which this is a true copy was served by me on the defendant personally at the address stated in the order, or at

on the   day of   19

                                                          Bailiff / Officer of the Court
                                                          Date

I certify that the order has **not been served** for the following reason:

                                                          Bailiff / Officer of the Court
                                                          Date

Figure 10.14 (reverse)

Request for Reissue of Enforcement or Oral Examination (not Warrant)

In the _____ County Court

Case Number

	Type of Process (Tick appropriate box and enter case number and number of process).		
☐	Attachment of earnings	A/E No.
☐	Oral examination	O/E No.
☐	Judgment summons	J/S No.
☐	Other _please specify, charging order, garnishee etc_	No.

1 Plaintiff's name.

2 Name and address for service and payment.

Ref./Tel. No.

3 Defendant's name and address.

For court use only

Hearing Date:

on

at   o'clock

at (address)

Reissue date:

I certify that (* the whole or part of any instalments due under the judgment or order have not been paid and that) the balance now due under this judgment is as shown († and that the amount due under the judgment summons is as shown at (B)).

4 Outstanding debt.

(A) Balance due* at date of this request (including costs of issue of post-judgment process and unsatisfied warrant costs)†.
  * including any interest to date of request where judgment is over £5,000 and is entered on or after 1 July 1991.
  † except where reissuing oral examination.

Unsatisfied warrant costs (oral examinations only).

(B) **Judgment summonses only.**
Amount due under the judgment summons (do not include amounts for which Defendant imprisoned).

Signed

Plaintiff (Plaintiff's Solicitor)

Dated

* Delete if you are applying to reissue an oral examination
† Delete if not applying to reissue judgment summons

IMPORTANT
You must inform the court immediately of any payments you receive after you have sent this request to the court.

Reasons for requesting reissue *(information you are relying on to support your application for reissue eg Defendant's address (or employment) has changed, he has failed to make payments under a suspended order etc.)*

Reissue No.

N446 Request for reissue of post-judgment process (other than warrant) (Order 25, rule 5(2))

OYEZ The Solicitors' Law Stationery Society Ltd. Oyez House, 7 Spa Road, London SE16 3QQ

County Court N446

1991 Edition 5.91 F19859

5039826

Figure 10.15 Request for re-issue of attachment

Request for Oral Examination

(to be completed and signed by the Plaintiff or his Solicitor and sent to the court with the appropriate fee)

1 Plaintiff's name and address.

In the

County Court

Case Number

2 Name and address for service and payment (if different from above). Ref./Tel. No.

For court use only

O/E No.

Issue date:

3 Defendant's name and address.

Hearing date:

on

at   o'clock

at (address)

4 Name and address of person to be orally examined if different from Box 3 (ie director of Defendant Company).

5 Judgment details

Court where judgment/order made if not court of issue

I apply for an order that the above Defendant (the officer of the Defendant Company named in Box 4) attend and be orally examined as to his (the Defendant Company's) financial circumstances and produce at the examination any relevant books or documents.

6 Outstanding debt

You may be able to claim interest if judgment entered for more than £5,000 on or after 1 July 1991

Balance of debt and any interest*/ damages at date of this request

Issue fee

AMOUNT NOW DUE

Unsatisfied warrant costs

I certify that the balance now due is as shown

Signed

Plaintiff (Plaintiff's solicitor)

Dated

IMPORTANT
You must inform the court immediately of any payments you receive after you have sent this request to the court.

N316 Request for oral examination (Order 25, rule 3(1A))

OYEZ The Solicitors' Law Stationery Society Ltd., Oyez House, 7 Spa Road, London SE16 3QQ

1991 Edition   5.91 F19882

5039333

County Court N316

Figure 10.16 Application for oral examination

Order for Oral Examination of Judgment Debtor

Plaintiff

Defendant

In the

County Court

Case No. *Always quote this*	
Oral Exam No.	
Plaintiff's Ref.	

To the defendant

The plaintiff obtained a judgment (or order)

(1) or as the case may be

against you in this court ( )(1)

(and (the plaintiff has not accepted the contents of your statement or affidavit)

(2) delete as appropriate

(or you have failed to provide a statement or affidavit as to your means or liabilities))(2)

Seal

You are ordered to attend before the district judge (or before one of the officers) of this court at the court office at

on at o'clock and be examined under oath as to your financial circumstances including what property or other assets you may have, and to produce at the examination any books or documents in your possession or power containing

(3) see note overleaf

information about your financial circumstances(3)

And it is further ordered that the costs of this application and of the examination be in the discretion of the district judge

Dated

This order was made on the application of

of

Plaintiff ('s solicitor)

Take notice: Repeated failure to attend an examination at the court may result in your imprisonment

(4) where judgment entered for more than £5000 on or after 1 July 1991

Balance of debt due at date of this request (and any interest) (4) £	
Fee on issue of this order £	
AMOUNT NOW DUE £	
Unsatisfied warrant costs not included above £	

Important - for instructions turn over

When corresponding with the court, please address forms and letters to the Chief Clerk and quote the case number.

The court office at

is open between 10 am and 4pm

N37 Order for oral examination of judgment debtor (Order 25, rule 3(1))

Figure 10.17 Order for oral examination N37

**How to Pay
and
Address for Payment**

- PAYMENT(S) MUST BE MADE to the person named at the address for payment, quoting their reference and the court case number.
- DO NOT bring or send payments to the court. THEY WILL NOT BE ACCEPTED.
- You should allow at least 4 days for your payment to reach the plaintiff or his representative.
- Make sure that you keep records and can account for all payments made. Proof may be required if there is any disagreement. It is not safe to send cash unless you use registered post.
- A leaflet giving further advice about payment can be obtained from the court.
- If you need more information you should contact the plaintiff or his representative.

Books or documents in your possession or power

When you attend the examination the court will expect you to provide evidence of your income and commitments. Examples of the sort of evidence you should bring with you are:

- rent books
- pay slips
- bank statements
- court orders on which you still owe money
- share certificates etc

- receipt for mortgage repayments
- hire-purchase or other hiring agreements
- Building Society, Post Office or Trustee Savings Bank books
- bills which you either owe or are owed to you

If you own, or are a partner in, a business you should also bring with you documents to prove the present financial state of the business.

Amount now due

It will not be necessary for you to attend the examination if you pay before the date of the hearing, the sum shown on the front of this form as the amount now due (see **How to Pay** above). If the plaintiff's claim includes interest and you pay the amount now due within 8 days of service of this order on you, the plaintiff will not be entitled to further interest. *(The date of service will be 7 days after the date of posting as shown by the postmark.)*

Note:

If payment is made too late to prevent the plaintiff's attendance at the hearing, you may be liable for further costs.

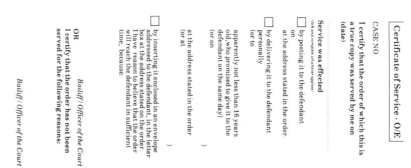

Figure 10.17 (continued)

Order for Oral Examination (person other than judgment debtor)

Plaintiff

| | In the |
| | |

Defendant

| | County Court |
| | |

Case No.	*Always quote this*	
Oral Exam No.		
Plaintiff's Ref.		

To the defendant   Seal

The plaintiff obtained a judgment (or order) against you in this court

(1) or as the case may be   (   )(1)

(and (the plaintiff has not accepted the contents of your statement or affidavit filed on behalf of the company) (or the company has failed to provide a statement or affidavit as to its means or liabilities))(1) and as it appears that you are an officer of the defendant company

You are ordered to attend before the district judge (or before one of the officers) of this court at the court office at

on   at   o'clock and be examined under oath as to the financial circumstances of the defendant company including what property or other assets it may have, and to produce at the examination any books or documents in your possession

(2) see note overleaf   or power containing information about the financial circumstances of the defendant company(2)

And it is further ordered that the costs of this application and of the examination be in the discretion of the district judge

Dated

This order was made on the application of

                                        of   Plaintiff ('s solicitor)

Take notice: Repeated failure to attend an examination at the court may result in your imprisonment

(3) where judgment entered for more than £5000 on or after 1 July 1991

Balance of debt due at date of this request (and any interest) (3) £	
Fee on issue of this order £	
AMOUNT NOW DUE £	

Unsatisfied warrant costs not included above £

Important - for instructions turn over

The court office at

is open between 10 am and 4pm Monday to Friday. When corresponding with the court, please address forms and letters to the Chief Clerk and quote the case number.

N38 Order for oral examination (person other than judgment debtor) (Order 25, rule 3(1))

Figure 10.18 Order for oral examination N38

How to Pay
and
Address for Payment

- **PAYMENT(S) MUST BE MADE to the person named at the address for payment, quoting their reference and the court case number.**
- **DO NOT bring or send payments to the court. THEY WILL NOT BE ACCEPTED.**
- You should allow <u>at least</u> 4 days for your payment to reach the plaintiff or his representative.
- Make sure that you keep records and can account for all payments made. Proof may be required if there is any disagreement. It is not safe to send cash unless you use registered post.
- A leaflet giving further advice about payment can be obtained from the court.
- If you need more information you should contact the plaintiff or his representative.

Books or documents in your possession or power

When you attend the examination, the court will expect you to provide information to prove the present financial state of the business. You should bring with you any relevant books or documents.

Amount now due

It will not be necessary for you to attend the examination if your company pays or causes to be paid before the date of the hearing, the sum shown on the front of this form as the amount now due (see **How to Pay** above). If the plaintiff's claim includes interest and you pay the amount due within 8 days of service of this order on you, the plaintiff will not be entitled to further interest.

(The date of service will be 7 days after the date of posting as shown by the postmark.)

Note:

If payment is made too late to prevent the plaintiff's attendance at the hearing, your company may be liable for further costs.

Certificate of Service - O/E

CASE NO.

I certify that the order of which this is a true copy was served by me on (date)

....

Service was effected
(tick and complete whichever applies)

☐ by posting it to the defendant on
at the address stated in the order.

☐ by delivering it to the defendant personally
(or to

apparently not less than 16 years old, who promised to give it to the defendant on the same day)
(or on

at the address stated in the order
(or at

by inserting it enclosed in an envelope addressed to the defendant, in the letter box at the address stated in the order.
I have reason to believe that the order will reach the defendant in sufficient time, because:

Bailiff / Officer of the Court

OR
I certify that the order has not been served for the following reasons:

Bailiff / Officer of the Court

Figure 10.18 (continued)

Order for (Defendant's) Attendance at Adjourned Oral Examination

To (the defendant)

In the		
		County Court
Case No. *Always quote this*		
Plaintiff		
Defendant		
Oral Exam No.		
Plaintiff's Ref.		

Seal

You were ordered to attend court on the   day of   19
at   o'clock to be examined under oath as to your financial circumstances
(or as to the financial circumstances of the defendant company) and you failed to do so

The appointment for your examination has been adjourned to
                         the   day of   19   , at   o'clock

at

when you are ordered to attend

And take notice that if you fail to do so you may be sent to prison for contempt of court

Dated

Travelling expenses

You are entitled to receive from the plaintiff a reasonable sum to cover your travelling expenses to and from the court. If you wish to claim these expenses you should write to the plaintiff's solicitor) at the address shown in the box below. You must write, stating the amount of such expenses, so that the plaintiff's solicitor) receives your claim not later than 7 days before the date of the adjourned hearing.

Note: If you do claim your travelling expenses they will be added to the balance due from you to the plaintiff and will be payable at the same time or by the same instalments as that balance is payable.

The plaintiff('s solicitor's) name and address is

Balance now due

You will not have to attend the examination if you (or your company) pay **into the court office** before the date of the hearing, the balance now due shown below

Note: If payment is made too late to prevent the plaintiff's attendance at the hearing, you (or your company) may be liable for further costs

Balance now due*
(including costs of the hearing which you failed to attend)   £

Unsatisfied warrant costs not included above   £

*Where judgment was entered for more than £5000 on or after 1 July 1991, the amount shown here may include interest to the date of the application. If so, the plaintiff may claim further interest until full payment.

**Important -
for instructions on what to bring to the hearing and how to pay, turn over.**

The court office at

is open between 10 am and 4 pm Monday to Friday. When corresponding with the court, please address forms or letters to the Chief Clerk and quote the case number.

N39 Order for defendant's attendance at an adjourned hearing of an oral examination (Order 25, rule 3(4))

Figure 10.19 Form N39

Books or documents in your possession or power

When you attend the examination the court will expect you to provide evidence of your income and commitments.

Examples of the sort of evidence you should bring with you are:

- rent books
- receipts for mortgage repayments
- pay slips
- hire-purchase or other hiring agreements
- bank statements
- Building Society, Post Office or Trustee Savings Bank books
- court orders on which you still owe money
- bills which you either owe or are owed to you
- share certificates etc

If you own, or are a partner in, a business you should also bring with you documents to prove the present financial state of the business.

Payments into Court

You can pay the court

by calling at the court office which is open 10 am to 4 pm Monday to Friday.
You may only pay by:

- cash
- banker's or giro draft
- cheque supported by a cheque card
- cheque (unsupported cheques may be accepted, subject to clearance, if the Chief Clerk agrees)

Cheques and drafts must be made payable to HM Paymaster General and crossed.
Please bring this form with you.

By post
You may only pay by:

- postal order
- banker's or giro draft
- cheque (cheques may be accepted, subject to clearance, if the Chief Clerk agrees)

The payment must be made out to HM Paymaster General and crossed.
This method of payment is at your own risk.
And you must:

- pay the postage
- enclose this form
- enclose a self addressed envelope so that the court can return this form with a receipt

*The court **cannot** accept stamps or payments by bank and giro credit transfers.*

Note: You should carefully check any future forms from the court to see if payments should be made directly to the plaintiff.

Certificate of Service (to be completed by the court)

I certify that the order of which this is a true copy was served by me on the within named personally at the address stated in the order, or at

on the   day of   19

Bailiff / Officer of the Court

Date

I certify that the order has **not been served** for the following reason:

Bailiff / Officer of the Court

Date

Figure 10.19 (continued)

Example 12   · An example of Form N349

IN THE   **COUNTY COURT**

                                                        CASE No.

BETWEEN   ....   PLAINTIFF

AND   ....   DEFENDANT

AND   ....   GARNISHEE

(1) Insert   I,(1)
full name,
address and
occupation
of deponent.

[Solicitor for] the above-named plaintiff, make oath and say:-

1. That I [or   ]
    on the   day of   19   , obtained a judgment [or an order] in this court against the
    above-named defendant for payment of the sum of £   for debt [or damages] and costs.

2. That £   is still due and unpaid under the judgment [or order].

3. That to the best of my information or belief the garnishee,

    of

(2) Add if   is indebted to the defendant [in the sum of £   ](2)
known   The grounds of my information or belief are: (state your grounds)

4. That the garnishee is a deposit taking institution having more than one place of business [and the
    name and address of the branch at which the defendant's account is believed to be held is:

    and the number of the account is believed to be   ] OR [I do not know
    at which branch the defendant's account is held, or what the number of the account is].

5. That the last known address of the defendant is:

    Sworn at   in the
                                          ⎫
           of   this   ⎬   _____
                                          ⎭
        day of   19

                                              Before me
                                              Officer of a Court, appointed by
                                              the Judge to take affidavits.

    This affidavit is filed on behalf of the plaintiff.

N.349 Affidavit in support of application for garnishee order Order 30 Rule 2.   MCR 035854/1/8136381 7m 5/88 L

Figure 10.20 Affidavit to support garnishee application

Garnishee Order to Show Cause

	In the
Plaintiff	
Defendant	**County Court**
Garnishee	Case No. *Always quote this*
To	Plaintiff's Ref.

Seal

On reading the affidavit of   filed on

It is ordered that the garnishee do attach so much of the debts owing or accruing from the said garnishee to the defendant as will satisfy a judgment or order obtained against the said defendant by the plaintiff on

(1) where judgment entered for more than £5000 on or after 1 July 1991

for the sum of £   including (any interest (1) and) costs, of which the sum of £ remains due and unpaid, together with £   the costs of these proceedings

And it is ordered that the garnishee do attend this court

at

on   at   o'clock

to give good reasons why an order should not be made that the garnishee do pay to the plaintiff the debt due from the garnishee to the defendant or so much of it as may be sufficient to satisfy the judgment or order, together with the costs of these proceedings

(2) delete if garnishee is not a deposit-taking institution

(2)(The garnishee may, at any time before the return day, give notice to the proper officer at the court that he does not hold any money to the credit of the defendant. The proceedings against the garnishee shall then be stayed.)

Amount of judgment (or order) (and any interest (1)) £	
Court fee £	
Solicitor's costs £	
Total £	**Dated**

(The name and address of the branch of the garnishee deposit-taking institution at which the defendant's account is believed to be held is:

(2)

Account No:

Defendant's name and address

Plaintiff's (solicitor's) address for service

The court office at

is open between 10 am and 4 pm Monday to Friday. When corresponding with the court please address forms or letters to the Chief Clerk and quote the case number.

N84 Garnishee order to show cause (Order 30, rule 3(1))

Figure 10.21 Garnishee order nisi

In the _____ County Court

Warrant of Committal

Case No. _____

Committal _____
Warrant _____
Number _____

Date applied for _____
Amount due under order £ _____

PLAINTIFF

Plaintiff(solicitor)'s address

Ref. _____
DEFENDANT

Returns other than payments

Date	Time			

I arrested the defendant on the

and delivered him into the custody of
the Governor of HM Prison at

on the

Bailiff

Amounts recovered or passed throug[1]

Date issued	Amount	Date issued	Amount	Amount

To the Governor of Her Majesty's Prison
at *(here insert name of prison of foreign court)*

(seal)

Take notice that, in accordance with the provisions of section 122 of the County Courts Act 1984, this warrant of committal has been sent to this court and the defendant, if arrested within the jurisdiction of this court, is to be conveyed to the prison of this court, and is to be kept there for the time mentioned in the warrant of committal or until lawfully discharged if sooner

Dated

N75 Indorsement on a warrant of committal sent to a foreign court (Order 28, rule 11(3))

To the district judge of the _____ **County Court**

(seal)

Take notice that this warrant has been issued out of this court for execution at an address within the jurisdiction of your court
You are therefore required to execute the said warrant

Dated

N53 Warrant of execution or committal to district judge of foreign court (section 122, County Courts Act 1984)

N74 Warrant of committal (Order 28, rule 11(1))

Figure 10.21 (continued)

Garnishee Order Absolute

Plaintiff	
Defendant	
Garnishee	

In the

County Court

Case No. *Always quote this*

Plaintiff's Ref.

Seal

To the garnishee

On hearing the plaintiff ('s solicitor) and the garnishee and reading the affidavit

of   filed on

and the order to show cause made on

when it was ordered that all debts due or accruing due from the garnishee to the defendant should

be attached to satisfy a judgment obtained against the defendant by the plaintiff in this court

on   for the sum of £   including

costs, of which the sum of £   remained due and unpaid (together with the costs of these

proceedings)

(1) where judgment entered for more than £5000 on or after 1 July 1991

It is therefore ordered that the garnishee do pay to the plaintiff the sum of £   , the

sum of £   , the debt due from the garnishee to the defendant (being so much of the debt

due from the garnishee to the defendant as is sufficient to satisfy the judgment debt and costs, together

(2) delete if garnishee owes less than the judgment debt, costs and costs of these proceedings

with any interest[1] and £   the costs of these proceedings) [2] to the plaintiff

by

(And that the sum of £   , the plaintiff's costs of this application, be added to the

judgment debt and be retained out of the money recovered by the plaintiff under this order and in

(3) delete if garnishee is able to satisfy the judgment debt, costs and costs of these proceedings

priority to the amount of the judgment debt) [3]

Dated

── **Address for Payment** ──	─────── **How to Pay** ───────
	• **PAYMENT(S) MUST BE MADE to** the person named at the address for payment quoting their reference and the court case number. • **DO NOT bring or send payments to the court. THEY WILL NOT BE ACCEPTED.** • You should allow <u>at least</u> 4 days for your payment to reach the plaintiff or his representative. • Make sure that you keep records and can account for all payments made. Proof may be required if there is any disagreement. It is not safe to send cash unless you use registered post. • A leaflet giving further advice about payment can be obtained from the court. • If you need more information you should contact the plaintiff or his representative.

The court office at

is open between 10 am and 4 pm Monday to Friday. When corresponding with the court, please address forms or letters to the Chief Clerk and quote the case number.

N85 Garnishee order absolute (Order 30, rule 7(1))

Figure 10.22 Garnishee order absolute

Case No.

Certificate of Service (garnishee)

I certify that the order of which this is a true copy was served by me on
(date) ....

Service was effected *(tick and complete whichever applies)*

☐ by posting it to the garnishee
on   at the address
stated in the order.

☐ by posting it to (leaving it at) the address stated in the
order as the registered office of the limited company.

☐ by posting it to (leaving it at) the address stated in the
order as the place of business of the limited company.

☐ by delivering it to the garnishee personally
(or to

apparently not less than 16 years old, who promised
to give it to the garnishee on the same day)
(or on   ) at the address
stated in the order (or at

☐ by inserting it, enclosed in an envelope addressed to
the garnishee, in the letter box at the address stated
in the order. I have reason to believe that the
order will reach the garnishee in sufficient time
because:

Bailiff / Officer of the Court

OR I certify that the order has not been served for the following
reason:

Bailiff / Officer of the Court

Certificate of Service (defendant)

I certify that the order of which this is a true copy was served by me on
(date) ....

Service was effected *(tick and complete whichever applies)*

☐ by posting it to the defendant
on   at the address
stated in the order.

☐ by posting it to (leaving it at) the address stated in the
order as the registered office of the limited company.

☐ by posting it to (leaving it at) the address stated in the
order as the place of business of the limited company.

☐ by delivering it to the defendant personally
(or to

apparently not less than 16 years old, who promised
to give it to the defendant on the same day)
(or on   ) at the address
stated in the order (or at

☐ by inserting it, enclosed in an envelope addressed to
the defendant, in the letter box at the address stated
in the order. I have reason to believe that the
order will reach the defendant in sufficient time
because:

Bailiff / Officer of the Court

OR I certify that the order has not been served for the following
reason:

Bailiff / Officer of the Court

Certificate of Service (garnishee's branch)

I certify that the order of which this is a true copy was served by me on
(date) ....

Service was effected *(tick and complete whichever applies)*

☐ by posting it to the garnishee's branch
on   at the address
stated in the order.

☐ by delivering it to the garnishee's branch personally
(or to

apparently not less than 16 years old, who promised
to give it to the garnishee's branch on the same day)
(or on   )
at the address stated in the order
(or at
)

☐ by inserting it, enclosed in an envelope addressed to
the garnishee's branch, in the letter box at the address stated
in the order. I have reason to believe that the
order will reach the garnishee's branch in sufficient time
because:

Bailiff / Officer of the Court

OR I certify that the order has not been served for the following
reason :

Bailiff / Officer of the Court

Certificate of Service (Order 7, rule 6(1)(a) and (2))

Figure 10.22 (continued)

Chapter 11

Other Enforcement Processes

A creditor who obtains judgment remains an "unsecured creditor". The judgment gives the creditor no priority over other unsecured creditors nor over the secured or preferential creditors (see Chapter 13 Insolvency). However, a charging order can give some "security" for the debt.

The bailiff or sheriff, in enforcing execution, is concerned with "goods and chattels" — basically items that are capable of being removed and sold. Thus, on seeking to enforce a judgment by execution, the plaintiff may be advised that the defendant has "No goods on which to levy". In such circumstances the plaintiff may know, or suspect, that the defendant owns his or her house or (the defendant being a limited company) owns an office block, factory, warehouse or piece of land.

Charging order

A charging order is a way of securing the debt against such an asset. Although they usually relate to land and buildings it is worth noting that other assets (eg government stock or stock of any body incorporated in England and Wales) can be secured in this way.

Of course, the plaintiff may not know with certainty that the defendant owns the property in question. Changes made by the **Land Registration (Official Services) Rules 1990** give any one a right to make a search at the Land Registry to ascertain the owner of land.

So, if the plaintiff knows the individual defendant's address or suspects that the corporate defendant owns the property it trades from, this can be confirmed by such a search.

A copy of the register relating to an address can be obtained for a fee of £7. For a fee of £13 an applicant can make a personal search of the register at the local Land Registry.

Not all land is registered but in future all sales of land and property will be subject to compulsory registration. Currently more than 13 million properties are registered. Search Forms are provided by the local Land Registry and the search may be made by post.

If the defendant is shown to be the owner of the property, then the plaintiff may decide to apply for a charging order. The process is one that is best dealt with by a solicitor. Indeed, if the plaintiff is a limited company and the debt is substantial, he or she will have to instruct solicitors (see Chapter 12 Court Rules and Orders).

The plaintiff prepares an affidavit, on similar lines to that for a garnishee application. It sets out the facts that:

(a) judgment was obtained by the plaintiff against the defendant on a given date for a fixed sum
(b) there is a balance due to the plaintiffs shown at the date of the affidavit
(c) the plaintiff believes the defendant to be the owner of the named property.

The affidavit asks the court to make a charging order over the property in respect of the debt, and names any other creditors (known to the plaintiff) who may be affected by the application.

On receiving the affidavit and the appropriate court fee the district judge will, if satisfied as to the facts, make a "charging order nisi", in effect a temporary charging order. This fixes a time and date for full consideration of the plaintiff's application and places an immediate charge (a mortgage) on the property until then.

Filing a "caution"

If the land is registered, the plaintiff must then register the order with the Land Registry by filing a "caution". This gives notice to the Land Registry of the charging order and warns it not to register any dealings with the land until the question of the plaintiff's charge has been determined.

The charging order nisi is served on the defendant who must then attend on the date fixed to "show cause" (give reasons) why the order should not be made absolute. The onus of proof is on the defendant to satisfy the court that the order should *not* be made absolute. However, the judge has wide discretion and may take into consideration the interests of other creditors and/or joint owners of the land or property.

If the order absolute is made, it gives the plaintiff a charge (mortgage) over the property in respect of the debt. The plaintiff may decide to take no further action but to "rest on his or her security" on the basis that if the defendant seeks to dispose of the property, any purchasers will want the charge removed (paid) before they complete the purchase.

The plaintiff may decide to apply for an order for sale of the property. This involves a fresh application to the court, by means of an originating application supported by an affidavit. It must be noted that if the plaintiff proceeds to force a sale of the property he or she must:

(a) sell it at the best market price available
(b) pay off, in full, any person or body who has a prior mortgage or charge on the property.

If there is a shortfall, in other words the sale price is not sufficient to pay off those holding prior mortgages or charges, then the plaintiff must make up the loss! (Obviously the plaintiff would ascertain in the legal process the value of such prior mortgages or charges before any sale.)

As can be seen the procedures are specialist and best dealt with by solicitors.

The appointment of a receiver

This method of enforcement is seldom used but it is worthy of mention. A plaintiff may have judgment against a defendant who has rents payable to him or her; has money due under a life assurance policy due to mature; has money in a joint account; has an income from a business or under a trust.

The application is made by affidavit and a notice of application. The plaintiff must nominate the person he or she wishes to act and the court must be satisfied as to his or her suitability.

The receiver will usually be an accountant or solicitor or some other professionally qualified person who will usually require to be paid. The plaintiff will be responsible for such payment and thus needs to be sure that the cost will be worth incurring.

If the plaintiff has obtained a charging order, he or she has the right to apply for a receiver to protect the proceeds of the sale of the land. Again, the question of costs needs to be carefully considered. This process is one in which the prudent plaintiff will seek immediate help from a solicitor.

Injunctions

In debt recovery actions, injunctions are rarely used. However, creditors may have reason to suspect that a debtor is concealing or disposing of assets to avoid meeting his or her liabilities.

A court can grant an injunction, before or after judgment. Thus, before an injunction can be granted an action must be commenced. The **Courts and Legal Services Act 1990** directs that "in any proceedings in a County Court the Court may make any order which could be made by the High Court if the proceedings were in the High Court". Thus, a plaintiff who has commenced an action in the county court for the recovery of a debt of any sum may, in appropriate circumstances, apply for an injunction. Two types of injunction in debt recovery actions are:

(a) a Mareva injunction
(b) an Anton Piller order.

Mareva injunction

This injunction can be applied for if there is a risk that the defendant's assets will be removed from England or Wales or will be in some way disposed of.

An application is made to a judge *ex parte*, that is without the defendant being given notice of it. It must be supported by a detailed affidavit. This must set out the grounds of the application and must show good grounds for the plaintiff's application (it must give reasons why the plaintiff believes that the defendant is removing or disposing of assets with a view to avoiding the consequences of the judgment).

In considering the matter the court will require the plaintiff to give an undertaking to pay damages to the defendant if the claim for the debt subsequently fails; the court may order the plaintiff to prove the ability to meet the undertaking and may order a sum of money to be paid into court by the plaintiff to support it.

If the injunction is granted the court will fix a date for the question to be fully considered, with the defendant having the opportunity to attend.

An Anton Piller order

This is an order enabling the plaintiff to enter premises to search for documents or property and to seize them. It is a process which the courts themselves regard as draconian and such orders are not made lightly.

Application is *ex parte*, supported by an affidavit. However, the burden of proof is on the plaintiff to prove a real prospect that the defendant may remove or destroy the documents or property. If the court is prepared to make the order, the plaintiff will be required to give an undertaking to pay damages if the claim should subsequently fail. The court will fix a date for a full hearing of the question, with the defendant being given the opportunity to attend. The plaintiff will also be ordered to serve copies of his or her evidence on the defendant prior to that hearing.

These procedures are complex and should never be attempted without the advice and assistance of a solicitor. They are seldom used in straightforward claims for debt and are mentioned here simply because they exist and plaintiffs need to be aware of them.

Further, where a Mareva injunction is sought in a county court action the application will be heard by a High Court judge. For this purpose the action will be temporarily transferred to the High Court (but only for the hearing of the application).

When an Anton Piller order is applied for in a county court action the *proceedings* will be transferred to the High Court. After the hearing of the application the proceedings will be referred back to the county court unless the High Court judge decides that it should continue in the High Court.

Chapter 12

Court Rules and Orders

This chapter deals with the rules which govern county court procedure. Although a plaintiff acting in person, without solicitors, is not required to be an expert on all the rules of the county court it must be appreciated that the county courts are part of the legal system. Thus their procedures are defined by a complex set of rules and orders. These are set out in *The County Court Practise* known as "The Green Book" which is published annually.

Matters set out in this book are dealt with by:

(a) the **County Courts Act 1984**
(b) the **Courts and Legal Services Act 1990**
(c) the **County Court (Amendment) Rules 1991**
(d) the **County Court (Amendment No. 2) Rules 1991**
(e) the **High Court and County Court Jurisdiction Order 1991**
(f) the **County Court (Forms) (Amendment) Rules 1991**
(g) the **County Court (Forms) (Amendment No. 2) Rules 1991**.

The County Courts Act 1984

Certain sections of this Act were repealed by the **Courts and Legal Services Act 1990**. However, all the remaining sections of the Act are in force, subject to some slight amendments.

The Courts and Legal Services Act 1990

This Act was passed in November 1990 and it:

(a) deals with the allocation of business between the High Court and the county court
(b) promotes the simplification of procedures
(c) seeks to improve the efficiency of the service provided to court users
(d) gives the county court unlimited jurisdiction in claims for debt
(e) gives the county court power to deal with personal injury actions involving claims up to £50,000
(f) directs that actions commenced in the High Court for claims up to £25,000 will, unless they are of particular importance or complexity, be referred to the county court for trial
(g) brings into operation the procedures outlined in this book.

In seeking to improve efficiency, the Act has taken some of the burden of administration away from court staff and placed it upon plaintiffs or their solicitors. Thus, plaintiffs will now prepare the summons; they will collect the money under summonses; offers and admissions will be sent by the defendant direct to the plaintiff (not via the court). In these ways the procedures in the county court have been made identical to those in the High Court.

The jurisdiction of district judges has been increased, enabling them to deal with defended actions involving sums up to £5000.

The County Court (Amendment) Rules 1991

The County Court (Amendment No. 2) Rules 1991

These rules bring into operation the provisions of the **Courts and Legal Services Act 1990** outlined above. Thus, once the Act of 1990 was passed into law it was necessary to amend the rules of the court so that the provisions of the Act could be implemented.

The High Court and County Court Jurisdiction Order 1991

This order, again, was necessary as a result of the changes promoted by the **Courts and Legal Services Act 1990**. It deals with the increase in the jurisdiction of the county court and the transfer of proceedings between courts.

It also defines the enforcement by execution provisions by directing that county court judgments for £5000 or more *must* be enforced via the sheriff and *may* be enforced for sums of £2000 or more. Below £2000 enforcement must be via the bailiff of the county court.

The County Court (Forms) (Amendment) Rules 1991

The County Court (Forms) (Amendment No. 2) Rules 1991

As appears from their title these two rules amended the forms used in the county court. All the court forms illustrated in this book are those prescribed by these rules.

Clearly this book cannot set out all the provisions of the Acts, rules and orders. However, all the steps and procedures outlined are in accordance with them. There are, however, some basic rules that should be understood.

The rule as to time for service of a summons

A summons must be served within four months of the date of issue (or six months if the summons is being served "out of the jurisdiction" (ie on a foreign debtor in a foreign country). Thus, the plaintiff must ensure that the summons is served within the time limits. Four months may seem a long time but, for example, service by post could result in the summons being returned marked "gone away". The plaintiff may then ask the bailiff to attempt personal service. More time passes and then the bailiff confirms that the defendant *has* left the last known address. The debt may be of sufficient value to

warrant the plaintiff taking steps to trace the whereabouts of the
defendant, but time is passing. The plaintiff then amends the summons, because he or she has a new address for the defendant, and
the bailiff attempts service.

The summons is of no effect if it is served *after* four months from
the date of issue. The rule concerning service says that "in exceptional
circumstances the Plaintiffs may apply for this time to be extended
provided that application is made before the Summons has expired".

Thus, if there is difficulty in serving the summons and time is
running out, the plaintiff must apply to extend the life of the summons. Application is by letter (quoting the case number), setting out
the facts.

The rule talks about "exceptional circumstances". Thus, the onus
is on the plaintiff to satisfy the court that there are good grounds
for extending the life of the summons. Thus, the plaintiff may write:
"The amount claimed is a substantial one and we have already
instructed our agents to make enquiries with a view to tracing the
defendant.

We anticipate their final report in two to three weeks and would
ask the court to extend the period within which service of the summons can be effected . . . ".

It is important to understand that an extension will not be granted
automatically and it is for the plaintiff to show "exceptional circumstances".

The "life" of the summons after service

The relevant rule specifies that:

> If the Plaintiffs do not ask for Judgment within 12 months of the date of
> service the action will be struck out. It cannot be re-instated.

Again, 12 months may seem a long time but plaintiffs must ensure
that they are not caught by this time limit.

If the defendant does not reply to the summons, the plaintiff
must apply for judgment. However, on receipt of the summons, the
defendant may contact the plaintiff and as a result the parties might
agree a settlement. For example, the plaintiff has sued for £2000 but
agrees that there should have been a credit note for £50, so the claim

is reduced to £1950. The defendant satisfies the plaintiff that the debt cannot be paid at once, and the plaintiff agrees to accept £150 per month. The defendant writes a letter confirming this offer and sends the cheques.

By now perhaps two months have passed since the summons was served. The plaintiff presents the cheques on their due dates and they clear, until cheque number ten. That is dishonoured and the plaintiff contacts the defendant, who states that the cheque will be honoured if it is represented. However, again the cheque is dishonoured.

The plaintiff now decides to apply for judgment for the balance due but the court will reject the application because the application is not "within twelve months of the date of issue". So far as the court is concerned nothing has happened for 12 months after the date of service so the summons has been "struck out". There *is* no summons before the court.

This rule makes it important for plaintiffs to ensure that all "arrangements" made with the defendant *after* the issue of the summons are dealt with "through the court".

With the summons, the defendant is given a set of documents to cover every eventuality. If he or she contacts the plaintiff and makes an acceptable offer to pay by instalments, the defendant should be advised to complete the admission and offer forms and send them to the plaintiff. The plaintiff advises the court that the offer is accepted by using the tear off section on Form N205A (Figure 4.1).

Now the court will enter judgment on the basis of the defendant's offer. The plaintiff can still accept post-dated cheques but *now* if a cheque is dishonoured, the plaintiff can enforce the judgment for the remaining balance. The same procedure can be used to deal with cases where the defendant contacts the plaintiff and admits only part of the debt. The plaintiff is prepared to accept it so, again, the defendant completes the admission and offer form admitting part of the debt. The plaintiff accepts the defendant's offer by completing Form N205A (Figure 4.1).

Again, the court enters judgment on that basis. If the defendant defaults in payment, then the plaintiff may apply to enforce the balance.

Some defendants may wish to avoid having a judgment entered against them. If so, they must make a proposal for payment in full *within* the 12 month period. The plaintiff may accept this proposal but, if any cheque is dishonoured or instalment not paid, he or she should, within the 12 month "life" of the summons, apply for judgment for the balance due at the date of the application.

Costs of arbitration hearings

As was shown in Chapter 5, arbitration is a procedure for dealing with claims up to £1000 (and up to £5000 with the consent of the parties) in the district judge's room in an informal way.

There is, however, a rule concerning "costs" on arbitration. If the plaintiff decides to instruct solicitors to represent him or her on a hearing, the court *cannot* order the defendant to pay more than is claimed in the summons. In other words, the defendant cannot be ordered to pay the costs of the solicitor for attending the hearing. The court can award the reasonable travel costs and expenses of witnesses.

Rights of audience

In the report of the Review Body on Civil Justice it was noted that the **County Courts Act 1984** gives rights of audience to barristers, solicitors and litigants in person. However, in this context it must be noted that a limited company is not a "litigant in person". In arbitration matters the district judge *may* allow an employee or officer of the company to conduct the case on behalf of the company. If, however, the district judge chooses to do so he may direct that the company must be represented by a solicitor. If a matter involving more than £5000 is defended, it will go to a hearing in open court. In such cases the plaintiff, if a limited company, *must* be represented by a solicitor and, if the solicitor does not undertake advocacy, by a barrister.

Devolution of district judges' functions to administrative staff

Where there is no basic dispute between the parties to an action the previous judicial function exercised by a district judge will be devolved to court administrative staff. The following functions are devolved:

(a) disposals
(b) suspension of warrants of execution
(c) variation orders
(d) attachment of earnings
(e) consent orders.

So far as disposals, suspensions and variations are concerned, clearly the only issue in dispute is the amount of the payments to be made by the defendant. Thus, these matters will be dealt with by the administrative staff of the court, thus releasing the district judge to deal with hearings.

With regard to attachment of earnings applications, again, administrative staff will deal with these. The minimum amount of debt that can be dealt with by attachment is £50.

Court staff will also be able to make orders by consent, without referring the matter to the district judge. The categories of consent order that can be dealt with in this way are:

(a) orders for payment of debt or a defined amount of damages
(b) orders for the return of goods
(c) orders for possession of land — other than land which includes residential premises.

Administrative staff cannot deal with consent orders when one of the parties to the action is a litigant in person. Thus, if the plaintiff in person submits a form of consent order signed by a defendant in person (see Chapter 9), the documents will be referred to a district judge. This will not necessarily involve a hearing; if the district judge is satisfied that the terms of the order are fair and reasonable he or she will make the order.

Administrative staff have the power to vary orders for payment on the request of either party and to suspend warrants of execution on application by the defendant.

Interest on county court judgments

As has been said, a plaintiff may include a claim in a summons for contractual or statutory interest.

When the claim is up to £5000, interest will stop on judgment. However, if the plaintiff has a judgment for £2000 or more, and elects to instruct the sheriff to enforce it by way of execution, then that is a High Court execution and interest will continue to run. Another order — **The County Court (Interest on Judgment Debts) Order 1991** stipulates that when a plaintiff requests enforcement of a sum which includes post-judgment interest the plaintiff simply includes the amount of interest in the balance. The plaintiff must also produce a certificate of:

(a) the amount of interest claimed and the sum on which it is claimed
(b) the dates from and to which interest is calculated
(c) the rate of interest.

On request, the court will provide the form of certificate to be completed and signed by the plaintiff.

Costs of abortive warrants of execution

A change introduced by the **Courts and Legal Services Act 1990** enables a plaintiff to recover fees (and any solicitors' scale costs) incurred on the issue of a warrant of execution which has proved abortive. Prior to this, these costs were not recoverable. As a result of the change, if a warrant proves abortive and the plaintiff adopts some other means of enforcement (eg oral examination) then the costs and fees of the abortive warrant can be added to the debt.

Administration orders

The report of the Review Body on Civil Justice proposed that this process should be expanded and improved. In essence it is a procedure that enables a debtor with multiple debts to apply to the court to consolidate them all and allow payment of a regular monthly sum to be distributed *pro rata* among all the creditors.

The **Courts and Legal Services Act 1990** adopted these proposals. The position now is that:

(a) any debtor may apply to the county court to make an administration order, whether there is a judgment against him or her or not

(b) any person or body having judgment against a debtor may apply for an administration order

(c) the court may, of its own volition, make such an order. Thus if a district judge is entering judgment against a defendant and it appears that the defendant owes considerable sums to other creditors which he or she is paying off, the judge may make an administration order, even though neither a plaintiff nor the defendant has requested it.

The debtor then files details of all his or her debts with the court. The district judge determines how much the debtor can afford to pay by instalments and makes an order to pay that sum to the court on a regular basis. The court then receives the payments and, in effect, administers the debtor's affairs. Creditors are notified of the order and cannot thereafter take any steps to enforce payment.

Further, if the court forms the view that the debtor is unlikely to be able to pay off the debts in full, it can order a "composition" which reduces the amount due to each creditor. A scheduled creditor who provides a continuing service to the debtor, in the nature of an essential utility, cannot withdraw that service without the leave of the court.

When considering making an administration order the court will decide whether a bankruptcy order would be more appropriate.

An administration order lasts for a maximum of three years. At the end of that period any creditor with a balance (or reduced balance) still due and owing may take enforcement action. If a debtor fails to pay the instalments due under an administration order the court may revoke the order. Then any creditor who wishes to do so may take enforcement action. Alternatively, the court may revoke the order and make another debarring the debtor from taking part in certain business activities for a maximum of two years. It may also debar the debtor from applying for credit unless the potential creditor is advised of the order.

The administration order procedure is designed to assist a debtor facing an intolerable debt burden to avoid bankruptcy but to discharge the debts by instalments over a period of time.

Evidence on arbitration hearings

As has been noted, if a claim is defended it will be transferred to the defendant's county court for hearing. If the claim is £1000 or less the matter will be dealt with by informal arbitration. This may mean that the plaintiff has to travel to various courts throughout England and Wales, involving both time and cost. The district judge has power, with the consent of both parties, to decide the case and make an order on the written statements lodged by the parties, without the need for them to attend. It must be noted that the consent of both parties is necessary. However, the forms of automatic directions (Figures 5.1 and 5.2) allow the parties to ask that "this case be decided on the written evidence only and without the parties' attendance".

As a first step the plaintiff might consider asking this. He or she should, at the same time write to the defendant asking him or her to consent to this on the basis that "This will save both of us the time and cost of attending the hearing. If you are not prepared to consent and it is necessary for our witnesses to attend we will, in the event of our obtaining judgment, apply for an order that you pay the reasonable travel costs of our witnesses. In support of such application we shall produce a copy of this letter to the district judge".

This may persuade the defendant to consent, but if not, then the plaintiff's witnesses must attend. If the plaintiff wins the case he or she can at least produce the copy letter to the court as evidence of an attempt to avoid incurring costs; he or she was willing to deal with the matter on written statements and it was only the defendant's failure to consent to this that led to the incurring of the expense of attending.

Obviously there will be cases which are too complex to deal with simply on written statements but, from an economic viewpoint, this method of dealing with arbitration hearings should be considered.

Chapter 13

The Insolvency Act 1986

Although not strictly an enforcement or debt collection method, any book concerning the recovery of trade debts must include some reference to this legislation. The **Insolvency Act 1986** made radical changes to the law concerning corporate and individual insolvency.

Corporate insolvency

The Act deals with insolvent companies, by placing an obligation on directors to take immediate steps to protect the creditors whenever insolvency arises or should reasonably be foreseen.

The steps to be taken are defined as four options open to the directors. They are:

(a) to put forward a supervised scheme — a creditors' voluntary arrangement or
(b) to apply to the court for an administration order
(c) to ask any debenture holder to appoint a receiver
(d) to resolve to put the company into creditors' voluntary liquidation.

It is a matter for the directors to decide which option they adopt, depending on the financial situation of the company.

Insolvency practitioner

Whichever option is chosen must involve the appointment of a qualified insolvency practitioner. His or her duty is to investigate the
conduct of every director or former director of the company and to
report to the Department of Trade and Industry. In particular, the
insolvency practitioner will be investigating:

1. What led to the insolvency?
2. When did the director know that the company was insolvent?
3. When *should* he or she have known?
4. Did he or she take *immediate* steps to protect the creditors?

There are two sanctions which can be imposed on a company
director:

(a) disqualification and
(b) personal liability for the debts of the company.

A company director who is disqualified may not take any part in the
management of any limited company for a minimum of two and a
maximum of 15 years.

Disqualification of a director can arise:

(a) on conviction for an indictable offence in connection with the
promotion, formation, management or liquidation of a company
(b) for persistent breach of the **Companies Act 1989** requiring any
return, account or other document to be filed with the Registrar
of Companies
(c) for failure to comply with the **Insolvency Act 1986** (eg failing
to exercise one of the available options)
(d) for fraudulent trading discovered in the course of a winding
up
(e) on insolvency, if his or her conduct as a director makes him
or her unfit to be concerned in the management of a company
(f) if, in the opinion of the Secretary of State for Trade and Industry, it is in the public interest
(g) if there is "wrongful trading".

Personal liability for the debts of the company may be imposed on a director responsible for "wrongful trading".

Wrongful trading

Wrongful trading arises when:

(a) a company has gone into insolvent liquidation and
(b) the individual director knew or ought to have known at some time before the commencement of the liquidation that there was no reasonable prospect that the company would avoid insolvent liquidation.

Thus the Act seeks to encourage company directors to comply with the law and take immediate steps to protect the creditors when insolvency arises or should be foreseen.

An insolvent company

A company is deemed to be unable to pay its debts:

(a) where a creditor (by assignment or otherwise) whose debt is more than £750 has served on the company, by leaving it at the company's registered office, a written demand (in the prescribed form) requiring the company to pay the debt and the company has for three weeks neglected to pay the debt or compound it to the reasonable satisfaction of the creditor, or
(b) where in England and Wales, execution or other process issued on a judgment, decree or order of any court in favour of a creditor is returned wholly or partly unsatisfied, or
(c) where in Scotland, the induciae of a charge for payment on an extract decree, or an extract registered bond, or an extract registered protest, have expired without payment being made, or
(d) where in Northern Ireland, a certificate of unenforceability has been granted in respect of a judgment against the company, or

(e) where it is proved to the satisfaction of the court that the
     company is unable to pay its debts as they fall due, or
(f) where it is proved to the satisfaction of the court that the value
     of the company's assets is less than the amount of its liabilities,
     taking into account its contingent and prospective liabilities.

Thus, the directors of a company in such circumstances are required,
by the **Insolvency Act 1986**, to take immediate steps to protect the
creditors, by exercising one of the four available options.

Each option involves the appointment of an insolvency practitioner
and an investigation. In broad terms these options work as follows.

A supervised scheme — a CVA

This option enables a company in financial difficulty to put forward
a formalised scheme to creditors to pay its debts in full, over a period,
or to compound its liabilities.

An insolvency practitioner is appointed and, in conjunction with
the directors, he or she draws up the scheme. The insolvency practitioner then applies to the court for leave to call a meeting of creditors
at a specified venue on a fixed date.

At the meeting the creditors may:

(a) approve the scheme
(b) amend the scheme
(c) reject the scheme
(d) approve or amend the scheme but nominate another insolvency
     practitioner.

Voting at the meeting is by debt value and any proposal requires a
majority in excess of three quarters of the value of debts of creditors
present and voting or voting by proxy.

If the proposal put forward is approved no creditor can:

(a) take any court action to recover or enforce payment of a debt
(b) present a petition for the compulsory winding up of the com-
     pany
(c) enforce any security or take back goods let to the company on
     lease, rental or hire

(d) take back goods sold under retention of title.

An administration order

If the company wishes to put forward a supervised scheme but it knows, or suspects, that some creditors have taken or intend to take action to sue for their money, or if a creditor has already taken enforcement action, then they may apply for an administration order.

The nominated insolvency practitioner applies to the court for an administration order. If the order is made then:

(a) all actions and enforcement procedures against the company are stayed
(b) no creditor may enforce any security against the company or take back goods subject to hire, lease, rental or retention of title.

The insolvency practitioner then calls a meeting of creditors to enable them to consider the scheme. Once again, approval requires a majority in excess of three quarters of debt value.

The appointment of a receiver

If the company has given a debenture to the bank to secure sums due to it, the directors may choose this option. They *ask* the bank to appoint a receiver.

The person appointed must be an insolvency practitioner and, under the **Insolvency Act 1986**, is known as an administrative receiver.

The administrative receiver's task is to manage the business and safeguard its assets with the intention of paying the sum due to the bank. He or she must also settle the claims of the preferential creditors. Once this task is completed the remaining assets will be returned to the company or to a liquidator.

Creditors' voluntary liquidation

In a situation where the company finds it cannot pay its creditors and wishes to proceed into creditors' voluntary liquidation, the company must, again, appoint an insolvency practitioner and then:

(a) call a meeting of creditors and give at least seven days' notice of the meeting
(b) advertise the meeting in the *London Gazette* and once in two newspapers circulating in the area of the company's principal place of business.

The notice of the meeting must state either:

(a) the name and address of an insolvency practitioner who will, prior to the meeting, furnish creditors, free of charge, with any reasonable information about the company or
(b) the address to which creditors can go to inspect a list of creditors.

The directors then prepare a statement of affairs for the creditors, supported by an affidavit and send proxy forms to each creditor with a notice of a meeting of creditors.

Despite the fact that the company has appointed an insolvency practitioner the creditors may, at the first meeting, appoint their own choice.

The nominated liquidator must:

(a) within 14 days of appointment publish a notice in the *London Gazette*
(b) give notice to the Registrar of Companies
(c) within seven days of the meeting of creditors, file a statement of affairs with the Registrar of Companies.

To ensure that the assets of the company remain intact until there has been a meeting of creditors, the **Insolvency Act 1986** directs that the insolvency practitioner may not dispose of any assets (other than perishables) before the meeting of creditors without leave of the court. Thus the assets of the company, other than perishables, will be retained until the meeting of creditors has confirmed the appointment of a liquidator.

The creditors have the right to appoint a committee of creditors to work with the insolvency practitioner. When the liquidation is complete, the insolvency practitioner files a final report with the Registrar of Companies.

The creditors' powers

Creditors retain the right to force a company into compulsory liquidation. A creditor may present a petition against a company which is unable to pay its debts as defined above.

The **Insolvency Act 1986** has created a prescribed form of written demand, known as a statutory demand for payment (Figure 13.1). The form does not need to be signed by a solicitor; it is not "issued" by a court. The creditor completes the form and "leaves it at the registered office of the company". Sending the demand by post will not do; it must be taken to and left at the registered office. It is important to ensure that the form is accurately completed and properly served.

The company has 21 days from the date of service to pay the debt, put forward proposals for payment or show grounds of genuine dispute.

Statutory demand

The service of the statutory demand is an allegation of insolvency and a threat to wind up the company. Thus the company faces some basic but serious decisions:

1. Is the company insolvent or not?
2. If it is not, the directors should arrange payment within the time limited.
3. If there is a "cash flow problem" the directors need to agree proposals for payment with the creditor.
4. If there is a genuine problem or query, the directors should seek to resolve it with the creditor.

If, however, the company ignores the statutory demand and the creditor presents a petition, the company directors face a more basic but serious decision: whether to pay the debt, or face the winding up of the company.

If they pay, they are responsible for the court fees, costs and interest. If they do not pay, the company will be wound up and the official receiver takes over. He or she is required to investigate the conduct of the directors. He or she also needs to enquire *when* the directors knew that the company was insolvent.

The service of the statutory demand alleged insolvency: was the company insolvent or not? If it was, the directors had a period of 21 days to comply with the **Insolvency Act 1986**, to take steps to protect the creditors. Why did they not do this? Are they potential candidates for personal liability and/or disqualification?

Sanctions

It must be understood that not every compulsory liquidation will lead to sanctions against the directors. However, the threat is there and the service of a statutory demand may well lead to the directors of the company putting forward proposals for payment.

County winding up order

The county has power to make a winding up order against a limited company whose registered office is within its district and whose paid up share capital does not exceed £120,000.

Individual insolvency — bankruptcy

The **Insolvency Act 1986** also deals with individual bankruptcy and gives the creditor the right to serve a statutory demand in respect of a judgment which is unsatisfied or in respect of a debt for £750 or more.

Thus, if a creditor has obtained judgment, instructed the bailiff and the bailiff reports: "No goods on which to levy" then the creditor may proceed with a bankruptcy petition.

Alternatively, if a creditor is owed £750 or more, the creditor may serve a statutory demand and, if that is ignored, may present a petition.

Statutory demand

There are two types of statutory demand that can be used against an individual:

(a) in respect of a debt due immediately (Figure 13.2)
(b) in respect of a debt payable at a future date (Figure 13.3).

Note that on this demand the creditor must insert the name and address of the court to which the debtor can apply to set the judgment aside. This will be the county court covering the district in which the debtor resides or trades.

Debt payable at a future date

The demand in respect of a debt due at a future date is only applicable to individuals. It would be appropriate in cases where a contract was made which required a customer to make "stage payments". If, before a payment was due, the creditor had good reason to believe that the customer would not be able to make the payment when it fell due such a demand could be served. The statutory demand must be served personally on the debtor.

The use of statutory demands

The threat to wind up a limited company or to make an individual bankrupt can be a powerful one. However, creditors should not use it indiscriminately. Before serving a statutory demand, a creditor should decide that if payment is not made as a result he or she will proceed with a petition. If the debtor "calls the bluff" and ignores the statutory demand and the creditor goes no further, the debtor knows he or she has bluffed successfully! There may be occasions when a bluff is justified but, if creditors want debtors to treat such demands seriously, they should regard them in the same way.

The presentation of a winding up petition or a petition in bankruptcy should be dealt with by the creditor's solicitors.

Statutory Demand
under section 123(1)(a)
or 222(1)(a) of the
Insolvency Act 1986
No. 4.1* (Rule 4.5)

> **WARNING**
>
> • This is an **important** document. This demand must be dealt with **within 21 days** after its service upon the company or a winding-up order could be made in respect of the company.
>
> • Please read the demand and notes carefully.

DEMAND

To

Address

This demand is served on you by the Creditor:

Name

Address

NOTES FOR CREDITOR

1. If the Creditor is entitled to the debt by way of assignment, details of the original Creditor and any intermediary assignees should be given in part B on page 3.

2. If the amount of debt includes interest not previously notified to the Company as included in its liability, details should be given, including the grounds upon which interest is charged. The amount of interest must be shown separately

3. Any other charge accruing due from time to time may be claimed. The amount or rate of the charge must be identified and the grounds on which it is claimed must be stated.

4. In either case the amount claimed must be limited to that which has accrued due at the date of the demand.

5. If signatory of the demand is a solicitor or other agent of the Creditor, the name of his/her firm should be given

The Creditor claims that the Company owes the sum of £   , full particulars of which are set out on page 2.

The Creditor demands that the Company do pay the above debt or secure or compound for it to the Creditor's satisfaction.

Signature of individual

Name
(BLOCK LETTERS)

Dated   19

*Position with or relationship to Creditor

*I am authorised to make this demand on the Creditor's behalf.
Address

Tel. No.   Ref No.

* Delete if signed by the Creditor himself

N.B. The person making this Demand must complete the whole of this page, page 2 and parts A and B (as applicable) on page 3.

1

[P.T.O

Figure 13.1 Statutory demand – limited company

Particulars of Debt (These particulars must include **(a)** when the debt was incurred, **(b)** the consideration for the debt (or if there is no consideration the way in which it arose) and **(c)** the amount due as at the date of this demand).

NOTES FOR CREDITOR

1. If the Creditor is entitled to the debt by way of assignment, details of the original Creditor and any intermediary assignees should be given in part B on page 3.

2. If the amount of debt includes interest not previously notified to the Company as included in its liability details should be given, including the grounds upon which interest is charged. The amount of interest must be shown separately.

3. Any other charge accruing due from time to time may be claimed. The amount or rate of the charge must be identified and the grounds on which it is claimed must be stated.

4. In either case the amount claimed must be limited to that which has accrued due at the date of the demand.

5. If signatory of the demand is a solicitor or other agent of the Creditor, the name of his/her firm should be given.

NOTE
If space is insufficient continue on reverse of page 3 and clearly indicate on this page that you are doing so

2

Figure 13.1 (continued)

Part A

The individual or individuals to whom any communication regarding this demand may be addressed is/are:

Name
(BLOCK LETTERS)

Address

Postcode

Telephone Number

Reference

Part B

For completion if the Creditor is entitled to the debt by way of assignment.

	Name	Date(s) of Assignment
Original Creditor		
Assignees		

How to comply with a Statutory Demand

If the Company wishes to avoid a winding-up Petition being presented it must pay the debt shown on page 1, particulars of which are set out on page 2 of this notice, within the period of **21 days** after its service upon the Company. Alternatively, the Company can attempt to come to a settlement with the Creditor. To do this the Company should:

● Inform the individual (or one of the individuals) named in Part A immediately that it is willing and able to offer security for the debt to the Creditor's satisfaction; *or*

● inform the individual (or one of the individuals) named in Part A immediately that it is willing and able to compound for the debt to the Creditor's satisfaction.

If the Company disputes the demand in whole or in part it should:

● contact the individual (or one of the individuals) named in Part A above immediately.

> **Remember! The Company has only 21 days after the date of service on it of this document before the Creditor may present a winding-up Petition.**

3

Figure 13.1 (continued)

OYEZ

Insolvency-Company 4.1*

Figure 13.1 (continued)

Form 6.1

Statutory Demand
under section 268(1)(a)
of the Insolvency
Act 1986.
Debt for Liquidated
Sum Payable
Immediately.
(Rule 6.1)

WARNING

- This is an **important** document. You should refer to the notes entitled "How to comply with a Statutory Demand or have it set aside".

- If you wish to have this Demand set aside you must make application to do so **within 18 days** from its service on you.

- If you do not apply to set aside **within 18 days** or otherwise deal with this Demand as set out in the notes **within 21 days** after its service on you, you could be made bankrupt and your property and goods taken away from you.

- Please read the Demand and notes carefully. If you are in any doubt about your position you should seek advice **immediately** from a solicitor or your nearest Citizens Advice Bureau.

NOTES FOR CREDITOR
- If the Creditor is entitled to the debt by way of assignment, details of the original Creditor and any intermediary assignees should be given in part C on page 3.
- If the amount of debt includes interest not previously notified to the Debtor as included in the Debtor's liability, details should be given, including the grounds upon which interest is charged. The amount of interest must be shown separately.
- Any other charge accruing due from time to time may be claimed. The amount or rate of the charge must be identified and the grounds on which it is claimed must be stated.
- In either case the amount claimed must be limited to that which has accrued due at the date of the Demand.
- If the Creditor holds any security the amount of debt should be the sum the Creditor is prepared to regard as unsecured for the purposes of this Demand. Brief details of the total debt should be included and the nature of the security and the value put upon it by the Creditor, as at the date of the Demand, must be specified.
- If signatory of the Demand is a solicitor or other agent of the Creditor, the name of his/her firm should be given.

* Delete if signed by the Creditor himself.

DEMAND

To

Address

This Demand is served on you by the Creditor:

Name

Address

The Creditor claims that you owe the sum of £
full particulars of which are set out on page 2, and that it is payable immediately and, to the extent of the sum demanded, is unsecured.

The Creditor demands that you pay the above debt or secure or compound for it to the Creditor's satisfaction.

[The Creditor making this Demand is a Minister of the Crown or a Government Department, and it is intended to present a Bankruptcy Petition in the High Court in London.] [Delete if inappropriate].

Signature of individual

Name
(BLOCK LETTERS)

Date   day of   19

*Position with or relationship to Creditor:
*I am authorised to make this Demand on the Creditor's behalf.

Address

Tel. No.   Ref. No.

N.B. The person making this Demand must complete the whole of pages 1, 2 and parts A, B and C (as applicable) on page 3.

I.P.T.O.

1

Figure 13.2 Statutory demand – individual

Particulars of Debt
(These particulars must include (a) when the debt was incurred (b) the consideration for the debt (or if there is no consideration the way in which it arose) and (c) the amount due as at the date of this demand).

NOTES FOR CREDITOR
● If the Creditor is entitled to the debt by way of assignment, details of the original Creditor and any intermediary assignees should be given in part C on page 3.
● If the amount of debt includes interest not previously notified to the Debtor as included in the Debtor's liability, details should be given, including the grounds upon which interest is charged. The amount of interest must be shown separately.
● Any other charge accruing due from time to time may be claimed. The amount or rate of the charge must be identified and the grounds on which it is claimed must be stated.
● In either case the amount claimed must be limited to that which has accrued due at the date of the Demand.
● If the Creditor holds any security the amount of debt should be the sum the Creditor is prepared to regard as unsecured for the purposes of this Demand. Brief details of the total debt should be included and the nature of the security and the value put upon it by the Creditor, as at the date of the Demand, must be specified.
● If signatory is a solicitor or other agent of the Creditor, the name of his/her firm should be given.

Note:
If space is insufficient continue on page 4 and clearly indicate on this page that you are doing so

Figure 13.2 (continued)

Part A

Appropriate Court for Setting Aside Demand

Rule 6.4(2) of the Insolvency Rules 1986 states that the appropriate Court is the Court to which you would have to present your own Bankruptcy Petition in accordance with Rule 6.40(1) and 6.40(2). In accordance with those rules on present information the appropriate Court is [the High Court of Justice] [County Court] (address)

Any application by you to set aside this Demand should be made to that Court.

Part B

The individual or individuals to whom any communication regarding this Demand may be addressed is/are:

Name...

(BLOCK LETTERS)

Address..

....

....

Telephone Number...

Reference..

Part C

For completion if the Creditor is entitled to the debt by way of assignment.

	Name	Date(s) of Assignment
Original Creditor		
Assignees		

How to comply with a Statutory Demand or have it set aside (ACT WITHIN 18 DAYS)

If you wish to avoid a Bankruptcy Petition being presented against you, you must pay the debt shown on page 1, particulars of which are set out on page 2 of this notice, within the period of **21 days** after its service upon you. Alternatively, you can attempt to come to a settlement with the Creditor. To do this you should:

● inform the individual (or one of the individuals) named in Part B above immediately that you are willing and able to offer security for the debt to the Creditor's satisfaction; or

● inform the individual (or one of the individuals) named in Part B above immediately that you are willing and able to compound for the debt to the Creditor's satisfaction.

If you dispute the Demand in whole or in part you should:
● contact the individual (or one of the individuals) named in Part B immediately.

If you consider that you have grounds to have this Demand set aside or if you do not quickly receive a satisfactory written reply from the individual named in Part B whom you have contacted you should **apply within 18 days** from the date of service of this Demand on you to the appropriate Court shown in Part A above to have the Demand set aside.

Any application to set aside the Demand (Form 6.4 in Schedule 4 of the Insolvency Rules 1986) should be made within 18 days from the date of service upon you and be supported by an Affidavit (Form 6.5 in Schedule 4 to those Rules) stating the grounds on which the Demand should be set aside. The forms may be obtained from the appropriate Court when you attend to make the application.

> **Remember:** From the date of service on you of this document:
> (a) you have only **18 days** to apply to the Court to have the Demand set aside, and
> (b) you have only **21 days** before the Creditor may present a Bankruptcy Petition.

3

Figure 13.2 (continued)

oyez The Solicitors' Law Stationery Society Ltd., Oyez House, 27 Crimscott Street, London SE1 5TS   1988 Edition 6.90 F17413

5090337

Insolvency-Bankruptcy 6.1   * * *

Figure 13.2 (continued)

Form 6.3

Statutory Demand
under Section 268(2)
of the
Insolvency Act 1986.
Debt Payable at
Future Date
(Rule 6.1)

WARNING

- This is an **important** document. You should refer to the notes entitled "How to comply with a Statutory Demand or have it set aside".
- If you wish to have this demand set aside you must make application to do so **within 18 days** from its service on you.
- If you do not apply to set aside **within 18 days** or otherwise deal with this Demand as set out in the notes **within 21 days** after its service on you, you could be made bankrupt and your property and goods taken away from you.
- Please read the Demand and notes carefully. If you are in any doubt about your position you should seek advice **immediately** from a solicitor or your nearest Citizens Advice Bureau.

NOTES FOR CREDITOR
- If the Creditor is entitled to the debt by way of assignment, details of the original Creditor and any intermediary assignees should be given in part C on page 3.
- If the amount of debt when due includes interest not previously notified to the Debtor as included in the Debtor's liability, details should be given, including the grounds upon which interest is charged. The amount of interest must be shown separately.
- Any other charge accruing due from time to time may be claimed. The amount or rate of the charge must be identified and the grounds on which it is claimed must be stated.
- In either case the amount claimed must be limited to that which will have accrued due when payment falls due on the date specified.
- If the Creditor holds any security the amount of debt should be the sum the Creditor is prepared to regard as unsecured for the purposes of this Demand. Brief details of the total debt should be included and the nature of the security and the value put upon it by the Creditor, as at the date of the Demand, must be specified.
- The grounds for the Creditor's opinion that the Debtor has no reasonable prospects of paying the debt when it falls due should be stated.
- If signatory of the Demand is a solicitor or other agent of the Creditor the name of his/her firm should be given.

* Delete if signed by the Creditor himself

DEMAND

To

Address

This Demand is served on you by the Creditor:

Name

Address

The Creditor claims that you will owe the sum of £

Full particulars of which are set out on page 2, when payment falls due on the   day of   19

The Creditor is of the opinion that you have no reasonable prospect of paying this debt when it falls due because:

.

[The Creditor making this Demand is a Minister of the Crown or Government Department, and it is intended to present a Bankruptcy Petition in the High Court of London.] [Delete if inappropriate.]

Signature of individual

Name
(BLOCK LETTERS)

Dated the   day of   19

*Position with or relationship to Creditor:
*I am authorised to make this Demand on the Creditor's behalf.

Address

Tel. No.   Ref. No.

N.B. The person making this Demand must complete the whole of pages 1, 2 and parts A, B and C (as applicable) on page 3.

[P.T.O.

1

Figure 13.3 Statutory demand – individual, future debt

Particulars of Debt (These particulars must include (a) when the debt was incurred (b) the consideration for the debt (or if there is no consideration the way in which it will arise) and (c) the amount of future debt and the date payment is due).

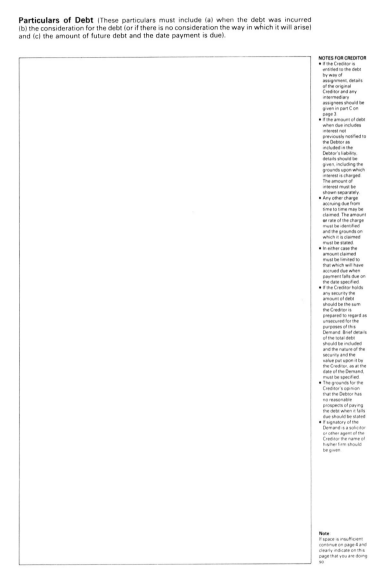

NOTES FOR CREDITOR

• If the Creditor is entitled to the debt by way of assignment, details of the original Creditor and any intermediary assignees should be given in part C on page 3.

• If the amount of debt when due includes interest not previously notified to the Debtor as included in the Debtor's liability, details should be given, including the grounds upon which interest is charged. The amount of interest must be shown separately.

• Any other charge accruing due from time to time may be claimed. The amount or rate of the charge must be identified and the grounds on which it is claimed must be stated.

• In either case the amount claimed must be limited to that which will have accrued due when payment falls due on the date specified.

• If the Creditor holds any security the amount of debt should be the sum the Creditor is prepared to regard as unsecured for the purposes of this Demand. Brief details of the total debt should be included and the nature of the security and the value put upon it by the Creditor, as at the date of the Demand, must be specified.

• The grounds for the Creditor's opinion that the Debtor has no reasonable prospects of paying the debt when it falls due should be stated.

• If signatory of the Demand is a solicitor or other agent of the Creditor the name of his/her firm should be given.

Note:
If space is insufficient continue on page 4 and clearly indicate on this page that you are doing so.

2

Figure 13.3 (continued)

Part A
Appropriate Court for Setting Aside Demand

Rule 6.4(2) of the Insolvency Rules 1986 states that the appropriate Court is the Court to which you would have to present your own Bankruptcy Petition in accordance with Rule 6.40(1) and 6.40(2). In accordance with those rules on present information the appropriate Court is [the High Court of Justice] [　　　　　　　　　　　　　　　　　Court] (address)

Any application by you to set aside this Demand should be made to that Court.

Part B

The individual or individuals to whom any communication regarding this Demand may be addressed is/are:

Name...
(BLOCK LETTERS)

Address..

....

....

Telephone Number..

Reference..

Part C

For completion if the Creditor is entitled to the debt by way of assignment.

	Name	Date(s) of Assignment
Original Creditor		
Assignees		

How to comply with a Statutory Demand or have it set aside (ACT WITHIN 18 DAYS)

If you wish to avoid a Bankruptcy Petition being presented against you, you must within the period of **21 days** after its service upon you, satisfy the Creditor that you are able to meet the debt demanded when it is due.

If you dispute that the debt will be due in whole or in part or if you dispute the allegation that you will be unable to pay the debt when it falls due or if you consider that you may be able to offer security for the debt or to compound for it you should:

• contact the individual (or one of the individuals) named in Part B immediately.

If you consider that you have grounds to have this Demand set aside or if you do not quickly receive a satisfactory written reply from the individual named in Part B whom you have contacted you should **apply within 18 days** from the date of service of this Demand on you to the appropriate Court shown in Part A above to have the Demand set aside.

Any application to set aside the Demand (Form 6.4 in Schedule 4 to the Insolvency Rules 1986) should be made within 18 days from the date of service upon you and be supported by an Affidavit (Form 6.5 in Schedule 4 to those Rules) stating the grounds on which the Demand should be set aside. The forms may be obtained from the appropriate Court when you attend to make the application.

> **Remember:** From the date of service on you of this document:
> (a) you have **only 18 days** to apply to the Court to have the Demand set aside, and
> (b) you have **only 21 days** before the Creditor may present a Bankruptcy Petition.

3

Figure 13.3 (continued)

oyez The Solicitors' Law Stationery Society plc, 24 Gray's Inn Road, London WC1X 8HR   1988 Edition   12 87 BM
5090028
Insolvency-Bankruptcy 6.3

Figure 13.3 (continued)

Chapter 14

The In-house Court Department

The increase in the value of debts that can be taken through the county court may encourage more businesses to undertake their own court work.

Some large organisations already have their own "in-house" county court department. Other businesses may be giving consideration to creating one.

The potential to reduce the costs paid to solicitors and the ability to retain day to day control over actions are benefits to consider. However, as has been shown in this book, the changes imposed by the **Courts and Legal Services Act 1990** mean that more of the administrative burden of court work is passed to the plaintiffs. Adequate, and adequately trained, staff will be required.

Again, the savings in solicitors' costs must be considered in the context of the cost and time incurred by using in-house staff.

A business faced with the need to issue a few county court summonses in the course of a year may well be able to delegate that task to its credit manager or controller. It will take up some time but should not create an impossible additional workload.

A business contemplating volume county court work must adopt a different approach. Volume work through the county court requires:

(a) adequate staff
(b) staff trained to understand the various court procedures
(c) a system for allocating cash and monitoring payments
(d) a good diary and filing system

(e) good documentation
(f) effective management by someone able to instruct solicitors
    and liaise with them as necessary.

Adequate and adequately trained staff

Volume issue of summonses will generate volume paper work. Summonses are prepared and issued; the court issues the summonses, confirms dates of issue and service and allocates case numbers. Dates must be put in a diary and case numbers noted on each file.

Then come the offers, payments, part offers, part payments, disputes in correspondence, defences, and defences and counterclaims. There will be notices of non-service as well as irate debtors on the telephone.

When defences are delivered the courts may issue automatic directions, which must be complied with within the time limited, or they may fix dates for pre-trial reviews. Meanwhile, a further batch of summonses has been issued and the cycle starts again. Sufficient staff to cope with these matters will be essential.

Training

Clearly, staff undertaking this work must have some basic training so that they understand the court system and its various procedures. One of the major problems a business faces in undertaking its own county court work is the lack of knowledge and understanding of the staff the work is delegated to. Certainly such staff do not need to be trained and qualified lawyers but they are working within the legal system and will certainly encounter lawyers (when instructed by defendants).

County court department

How the county court department is structured is a matter for the individual business. For example, are staff expected to issue summonses and carry those particular cases to a conclusion, whatever the defendants' response? If so, staff will *all* have to be capable of dealing with *all* aspects of county court work and procedure.

As an alternative, the work could be divided up so that:

(a) one person (or section) issues summonses, deals with admissions and offers, and deals with judgment in default and enforcement
(b) another person (or section) might take over the defended cases and take them to a conclusion, instructing solicitors as and when necessary
(c) there would be a manager to supervise and direct the total function.

This method enables staff with appropriate levels of knowledge to undertake specific functions.

Such issues need to be considered carefully and decided before bulk county court work is undertaken. The "bulk issue" facility offered by the county court is a great advantage to businesses concerned with volume work. It must be appreciated, however, that bulk issue will generate a bulk response, which must be coped with.

Systems for allocating cash and monitoring payments

The service of a summons will, in many cases, generate payments or part payments. Systems need to be established to allocate payments to the correct defendant, to ensure that judgments are entered for the correct balance of debt, court fee and interest. As is noted on all court forms relating to enforcement, the court must be notified *immediately* of any payments received *after enforcement process has been issued*.

A good diary and filing system

Both these elements are essential to the success of the county court function. Dates on which applications for judgment can be made must be entered in a diary as soon as the court advises the date of service. Dates for hearings must be noted as well as dates for follow up on correspondence.

A good filing system must be established so that copy summonses, defences and correspondence can be quickly referred to and so that incoming correspondence and paperwork is rapidly allocated to the correct file. Each file should contain a record sheet with information about the debt value, interest and court fees, and any enforcement action taken. In this way the current position of a case can be ascertained quickly so as to facilitate telephone conversations with the defendant or the court.

Good documentation

It is essential to standardise as much documentation as possible and to ensure that it is well prepared and presented.

It may, for example, be possible to pre-prepare all court forms so that the plaintiff's name and address, the wording of the claim and the claim for interest are already on the form. Then, to issue a summons involves only the insertion of the defendant's name and address, the figure for the claim and interest, and the court fee.

When it is necessary to lodge witness statements they should be typed on plain white A4 paper and headed in the action. They must be signed and dated. If copy invoices are produced they must be good, clean and readable copies.

Well presented and clearly laid out documentation is essential. The court officers and district judge need to be able to read documents presented to them. Poor quality, blackened photocopies do not help or impress them.

When lodging copy documents with the court, put them in date order and attach a front sheet headed with the action, quoting the case number and marked "Plaintiff's Documents". If there are a large number of documents, number them so that in witness statements or in presenting the case, reference can be made to, say, "document number six in the plaintiff's documents".

If it becomes necessary to instruct solicitors to attend a hearing, provide them with good copies of all the documents, including the summons and the defence.

Careful preparation of documents is an essential part of preparing the case for hearing.

The county courts are not a debt collection agency but part of the legal system; they are entitled to have cases properly presented to them to enable them to make decisions.

Effective management

The person responsible for the management of the department will need a good basic understanding of the legal system and will inevitably become involved in working with solicitors on complex cases. Indeed, one of the requisite skills will be to determine when solicitors need to be instructed.

It must also be appreciated that the manager may be required to conduct hearings before the district judge. Therefore he or she must be able to represent the business adequately, understand the rules of the court and be able to present a case in a logical way.

Resources

A number of large businesses do their own county court work very successfully. They have, however, allocated sufficient resources to it.

Some of them use specialist computer systems designed to produce summonses, judgments and enforcement documents, to provide a diary system, calculate interest and provide reports as and when required.

Many firms of solicitors which deal with volume court work have such computer systems and they can undoubtedly ease the administrative burden of the work. However, the computer cannot attend hearings or prepare for defended hearings and there is still a need for people with the expertise to deal with these aspects of court action.

Court attendances

It has been shown in earlier chapters that there are several types of hearing that may involve attendance at court. They are:

(a) informal arbitration
(b) disposals, when the parties cannot agree on the level of instalment payments
(c) pre-trial reviews
(d) applications for summary judgment
(e) hearings of claims up to £5000 before the district judge
(f) hearings in open court.

Accepting that where a complex dispute develops and in cases which go to open court solicitors are instructed, this means that the manager and some staff in the county court department will be involved in attending on the other types of hearing.

It is in the nature of volume county court actions that there *will* be cases where defences are delivered and these various types of hearing will arise. Add to this the fact that defended cases will be transferred to the defendant's court for hearing (and for pre-trial review) and it can be seen that some travel may be involved.

It is obviously going to be in the interests of the plaintiff to minimise the number of hearings attended. Such hearings will take up staff time and involve the plaintiff in travel and other expense. It may also be in the interests of a defendant who may, if the plaintiff succeeds in the claim, be responsible for the travel costs the plaintiff has incurred.

Consideration should be given to the following ways of minimising attendance.

Informal arbitration

As mentioned in Chapter 12, there is a facility for the district judge to deal with an arbitration hearing on the written statements and documents lodged with the court and without the need for the parties to attend. Plaintiffs should seek to use this procedure whenever appropriate.

Most small debt recovery actions are decided on the facts, not on any major point of law so there is not likely to be any detailed legal argument needed.

If the plaintiff's witness statements deal adequately with the points raised in the defence and if he or she has good documentation proving the order and delivery of the goods or services in dispute there is, perhaps, little to be gained by attendance.

As was noted, the district judge can only deal with the matter in this way with the consent of *both* parties to the action. The plaintiff should, whenever the case is suitable, seek that consent, by writing to the defendant on the lines suggested in Chapter 12.

If such consent is refused by the defendant then the plaintiff should attend. However, if he or she succeeds in the claim, it is possible to ask the district judge to allow a claim for reasonable travel expenses against the defendant.

If the plaintiff faces a defence and a counterclaim, it will be in his or her best interests to attend the hearing rather than simply relying on written statements.

Disposals

These hearings will only arise when the defendant admits the debt and offers to pay by instalments but the plaintiff rejects the instalment proposal.

The issue will then be determined, in the absence of the parties, by a court officer who will advise the parties of the order he or she is making. It is only if such order is not accepted by either party that a disposal hearing will be fixed before the district judge.

Thus, in considering an offer by the defendant, the plaintiff must look at the consequences of rejecting it. Time will pass before the court officer makes a decision and advises the parties; either party can object within 14 days. If an objection is received, a date for disposal will be arranged for some weeks ahead, and the plaintiff must attend or be represented. Thus the plaintiff must consider:

1. Is the offer reasonable in the context of the debt value and the defendant's financial position?
2. Is there information which, on a disposal, would convince a district judge to make a better order?
3. What will it cost to travel to the court?
4. Would it be more cost effective to instruct a solicitor to attend the disposal on behalf of the plaintiff?

Considering these questions may reduce the number of attendances on disposal hearings. The plaintiff could, if he or she wished to do so, instruct a local solicitor to attend the court and deal with the hearing on his or her behalf (see Chapter 15).

Pre-trial reviews

If the court does not issue automatic instructions, it will fix a date for a pre-trial review. This will take place in the defendant's court which will involve more travel and expense for the plaintiff. There are two ways of dealing with the problem *without* attending:

(a) instruct solicitors in the locality of the county court to attend the hearing (see Chapter 15) or
(b) ask the court to deal with the matter in the plaintiff's absence and give directions for trial.

If the plaintiff wishes to adopt the second option it is done by letter on the lines of Figure 14.1. The wording can be adapted to meet the needs of the case. For example, the plaintiff might want to ask that: "The district judge to be asked to decide the case on the written evidence lodged by the parties". Thus, the plaintiff has not only dealt with the pre-trial review hearing but has also asked the court, once a date for the hearing of the case is fixed, to deal with the matter on written statements.

The court is not obliged to deal with the matter by letter and can, if it feels it right to do so, require the parties to attend the pre-trial review.

However, if the plaintiff adopts the letter approach in appropriate cases the worst that is likely to happen is that the district judge will adjourn the pre-trial review, fix a further date and direct the parties to attend.

Applications for summary judgment

These will require attendance. Again, having prepared for the hearing the plaintiff can, if it makes economic sense, instruct a local solicitor to attend (see Chapter 15).

Hearings of claims up to £5000 — district judge

Again, attendance will be necessary, unless the matter is dealt with by arbitration and the parties agree to have the matter resolved on written statements.

When a defence has been delivered and a pre-trial review date fixed, the plaintiff could, for example, deal with the pre-trial review by letter and ask for the hearing to be resolved by arbitration on written statements.

The higher the debt value perhaps, the more economic it becomes to attend hearings such as this and the more complex such a hearing becomes. Nevertheless there may be cases where this procedure to avoid attendance can be adopted.

Open court and complex cases

Cases which are referred to open court for hearing and those where a complex dispute arises should be referred to solicitors. Indeed, if the plaintiff is a limited company it will be directed, on the pre-trial review, to instruct solicitors on the hearing.

As can be seen, the major problems the in house court department faces are those of staff levels and knowledge, and court attendances. By following the guidelines in this chapter the need for court attendances can be kept to a practical level. There will be occasions when solicitors must be instructed and we will consider working with them in the next chapter.

To: The Chief Clerk
      County Court

Dear Sir,

Ourselves and J. Debtor. Case No. _____
Pre-Trial Review date: _____

We refer to the above Pre-Trial-Review and would ask the Court
to deal with it in our absence. We intend no discourtesy to the
Court but simply wish to minimise costs.

We would ask for the following directions:
1. Parties to exchange and lodge witness statements within 14
    days of Order.

2. Parties to exchange and lodge documents within 14 days of
    Order.

We intend to call (two) witnesses and would ask the Court to:

a) Give the above directions.

b) Give such other directions as the Court consider
    appropriate.

c) Fix a date for hearing.

We are sending a copy of this letter to the Defendant.

Yours faithfully,

Figure 14.1 Suggested letter to court on pre-trial review

Chapter 15

Working with Solicitors

There will be cases in which it will be necessary to instruct solicitors. As shown in Chapter 14, there may be occasions when instructing a local solicitor may be more economic than travelling to the defendant's court to deal with certain types of hearing.

Not all solicitors undertake court work; some specialise in it. The automatic transfer of defended actions to the defendant's court may create a need to build up a list of solicitors to deal with claims in various courts.

Plaintiffs can, of course, telephone a firm and enquire whether it undertakes court attendances. Although the court staff cannot "recommend" a firm, they may be prepared to give the name of one or two firms which regularly appear in their court.

Solicitors charge for their time and expertise, so plaintiffs can save money by presenting them with well prepared and documented cases. The title of this chapter is "Working With Solicitors" and it encapsulates the relationship that produces the best results. Work with them, rather than using them. The "file of papers herewith — please attend" approach is not recommended.

The effectiveness and success of any solicitor involved in debt collection depends on three basic factors already dealt with in this book.

(a) the quality of the debt
(b) the ability of the client (the plaintiff) to prove the claim
(c) the ability of the defendant to pay any sum awarded.

The final and essential factor is good liaison between solicitor and client: clear instructions given in good time; prompt responses to questions raised by the solicitor; quick decisions on situations which may arise in the course of an action.

Clear instructions

Up to the stage of receiving instructions the solicitor knows nothing of the case. Whilst he or she does not need a long and detailed history of the defendant it is necessary to provide the relevant facts of the case, the documents and instructions as to what the plaintiff requires.

Instructions given in good time

Usually the court will give the parties reasonable notice of dates for hearings. Once a working relationship with a particular firm of solicitors has been established it will often be sufficient to send instructions without a prior telephone call. However, if there is a sudden urgent hearing, or if the plaintiff is seeking a solicitor to attend a hearing in an area where he or she has no regular contact, it makes sense to telephone first. The plaintiff can then confirm that the solicitor can deal with the case; if not he or she may provide the name of another firm which can.

Prompt responses to questions

The solicitor may raise questions or ask for clarification of certain points. A prompt response is essential. It is equally important that the response addresses the question asked and provides a reasoned answer. For example, a defended action is referred to a solicitor who is asked to attend the hearing of the case. The defendant is disputing the claim on the grounds that the price charged was too high and was more than that originally quoted. The solicitor writes:

> The defendant alleges the price he was quoted was considerably less than the amount of your final bill.

(a) What price was he quoted?
(b) Who by?
(c) Will that person be attending the hearing?
(d) If so it would be helpful to have a statement from that person.

The plaintiff's response: "He was quoted exactly what we charged" does not help at all. It is simply a repetition of the question which is in dispute. The plaintiff has ignored the relevant questions about what *evidence* there may (or may not) be to support what he or she is saying.

Prompt decisions

Situations will arise in which a solicitor needs "instructions" (needs the client to make a decision). The fact that a solicitor is instructed does not alter the fact that it is the plaintiff's case. The solicitor cannot agree matters with the other party or the solicitors for the other party unless he or she is told, by his or her client, to do so.

For example, the day before an action is due to be heard the defendant, or his or her solicitors, make an offer. They deny liability for the amount claimed but they are prepared to agree 65 per cent of it and the defendant wants to pay that sum, plus appropriate interest by three equal monthly instalments. The defendant is not prepared to pay any legal costs or fees.

The plaintiff's solicitor must put that to the client, and obtain instructions. The solicitor will certainly advise the client about the options and the benefits and disadvantages of each of them, but it is for the plaintiff to decide. In a company, whoever is delegated to do this needs the authority to make this sort of decision.

Types of hearing that may involve solicitors

Plaintiffs undertaking their own court work may find the need to instruct solicitors on various types of hearing. The need may arise on economic grounds — to avoid the plaintiff's representative travelling a long distance to the defendant's court. It may arise on the grounds of the legal complexity of the case.

As has been shown in previous chapters there are some hearings on which solicitors must be instructed and there will be other cases where it is economic or prudent to instruct a solicitor. Hearings on which a solicitor may be instructed include:

(a) pre-trial review
(b) interim applications (eg an application that the defendant should deliver further and better particulars of the defence)
(c) arbitrations
(d) defended actions not referred to arbitration
(e) applications for summary judgment.

Pre-trial review and interim applications

The plaintiff may wish the solicitor simply to deal with this aspect of the case. He or she may feel able to attend the actual trial of the case without being represented. This is perfectly acceptable and, once the solicitor has dealt with the particular hearing on which he or she was instructed, the papers will be returned to the plaintiff with a bill for the work done.

The solicitor will need a copy of the summons, the defence and copies of all the relevant documents.

Take the example of a defended action. The plaintiff has delivered a request for further and better particulars of the defence; the defendant has ignored the request and the date for the pre-trial review has been fixed. The plaintiff decides to instruct solicitors. It is necessary to provide copy documents, setting out the directions he or she wants the court to give and to ask the solicitor to attend. As it is a pre-trial review, the plaintiff's representative is not required to attend as a solicitor will represent the plaintiff.

The plaintiff writes a letter to the solicitor concerned, along the lines of Figure 15.1. The solicitor will deal with the hearing of the pre-trial review, report the outcome and return the papers, with a bill, to the plaintiff. It is now for the plaintiff to deal with the further steps in the action, attend the hearing of the action and arrange for the witnesses to meet the solicitor at the court.

Arbitrations — defended actions not referred to arbitration

A letter along the lines of Figure 15.1 can be used but as well as the papers listed in that suggested letter the plaintiff must:

(a) include copy witness statements
(b) provide a complete set of all the documents
(c) deal with any allegations raised in the defence, eg

> The defendant alleges that he was quoted a lower price than we are claiming. A verbal quotation was given by our Sales Manager Mr. Simon Jones. As you will see from his statement he did quote the price claimed and that price was confirmed by him in writing on the same day (document No. 5 in the bundle of correspondence). Mr. Jones will be at court to give evidence as outlined in his statement.

The solicitor then has all the facts and documents. He or she can very quickly understand the claim, review the evidence and prepare for the hearing.

The plaintiff must, of course, ensure that the witnesses are at the court in good time for the hearing. Usually the solicitor will want to spend some time with them going over the facts before the case comes on for hearing.

Applications for summary judgment

On these hearings it may be that the plaintiff will attend without solicitors. However if, because it is defended, the case is transferred to the defendant's court, the plaintiff may wish to instruct a local solicitor. For example, the plaintiff is in the south of England. He or she sues a defendant who delivers a spurious defence, but the case is automatically transferred to the defendant's county court in Newcastle-upon-Tyne.

The plaintiff prepares an affidavit and proceeds as outlined in Chapter 8. The Newcastle court fixes a date for the hearing of the application for summary judgment at 2.15 pm on a Friday.

The plaintiff's representative does not want to travel to Newcastle, so a solicitor is instructed (Figure 15.1 adapted as necessary) and the plaintiff includes all the documents listed in that example and includes a copy of the affidavit and any exhibits. The solicitor is asked to attend and: "Apply for summary judgment on the facts set out in my affidavit and supported by the documents exhibited".

By working with solicitors along these proposed lines the plaintiff can secure many of the benefits of the DIY method whilst having expert attendances on those hearings when it is necessary.

Plaintiffs who seek to *use* solicitors — (those who simply send documents a day or so before the hearing, leaving him or her to sort out the mess) will find their success rate is low. Further, they may find that a solicitor who has experienced the way the plaintiff works declines future business.

Dear Sirs,

Ourselves and Joseph Debtor — trading as _____
J. Debtor & Co. — Case No. _____ _____

We shall be obliged if you will attend the Pre-Trial-Review in this matter on   19   on our behalf. The hearing will take place in the   County Court.

We enclose:

i)   Copy Summons.
ii)   Copy Defence.
iii)   Copy Request for Further and Better Particulars of Defences dated _____ .
iv)   Copy Invoices.
v)   Copy Correspondence.
vi)   Notice of hearing — Pre-Trial-Review.

Our claim is in respect of (building materials) sold and delivered to the Defendant and is set out in the Summons, a copy of which is herewith.

As you will see from the Defence the Defendant alleges that "some of the goods were defective". On   we applied for Further and Better Particulars of this allegation. As at today there has been no reply from the Defendant.

On the hearing of the action we intend to call two witnesses.

We would ask you to attend on the Pre-Trial-Review and ask for an Order as follows:

a)   Defendant to deliver the requested Further and Better Particulars of Defence within 14 days or be debarred from Defending.

b)   Parties exchange documents and witness statements within 14 days.

c)   A date for the hearing of the action be fixed on the Plaintiffs written request.

Please advise us of the Order made on the hearing and, at the same time, return our papers together with a note of your charges.

Yours faithfully,

Figure 15.1 Suggested wording of letter instructing a solicitor to attend a pre-trial review

Chapter 16

Money Matters

Creditors taking action in the courts must bear in mind the cost implications. Issuing proceedings costs money, as does instructing solicitors, and the creditor:

(a) pays court fees in advance
(b) pays his or her solicitor's costs, win or lose.

Court fees

Court fees are sums of money charged by the court for the issue of various processes. They are payable at the time of issue and are added to the debt and thus payable by the defendant, provided that the plaintiff "wins". Current court fees are set out in Appendix 2.

Solicitor's costs

A creditor who instructs a solicitor to act is responsible for paying the solicitor's costs (the money the solicitor charges for his or her work).

Those costs are based on:

(a) the solicitor's expertise
(b) the value of the matter to the client
(c) the time spent by the solicitor.

Thus, most solicitors charge an "hourly rate". This may be £87.50 per hour for an assistant solicitor and £150 per hour (or more) for a partner. This charge is not simply for the time the solicitor spends in court but for the time he or she spends working on the matter.

This will include time spent reading the papers, considering the facts and the relevant law, drafting documents and writing letters.

Many creditors assume that if they win their case then the costs will be payable by the debtor. Whilst that is a basic general principle it must be understood that the court has total discretion with regard to costs. In other words it has power, when making a decision, to decide who pays the costs. It may direct that the defendant pays the costs "on the scale". The court may direct that there be "no order as to costs"; or may order the defendant to pay the plaintiff's costs "to be taxed".

Costs "on the scale"

The County Court Rules lay down a scale of costs, based on the debt value, which a solicitor may charge against the defendant for taking various steps in the action.

For example, the scale costs a solicitor may charge against the defendant for certain steps in the action are as follows:

On issuing a summons for service by the court

Debt value:	£25–£250	£250–£600	£600–£2000	£2000+
Solicitor's costs:	£24	£32	£54	£59

On entering judgment in default

Debt value:	£25–£600	£600–£3000	£3000+
Solicitor's costs:	£8.50	£16	£17.75

On judgment by accepting an offer

Debt value:	£25–£600	£600–£3000	£3000+
Solicitor's costs:	£15	£31.50	£37

On judgment on a disposal hearing

Debt value:	£25–£600	£600–£3000	£3000+
Solicitor's costs:	£20.25	£40.25	£47.50

On summary judgment

Debt value:	£500–£3000	£3000+
Solicitor's costs:	£69.50	£79.50

Charges for other steps in an action are laid down on the scale and these are the fixed costs recoverable from the defendant. The solicitor is, of course, entitled to charge the creditor (his or her client) for the steps taken, based on the criteria of time spent, expertise involved and value of the matter to the client.

For example, for preparing and attending on an application for summary judgment relating to a debt of £3500 the solicitor can recover scale costs of £79.50 from the defendant. Taking account of his or her time and expertise, the solicitor may assess the charges at £175, £79.50 from the defendant and £95.50 from the client.

Of course, if the defendant does not, or cannot, pay the £79.50, the client owes the solicitor £150.

"No order" as to costs

If the court makes no order as to costs then the rule is that each side pays its own costs.

Costs "to be taxed"

After a trial, the court may direct that the defendant pays the plaintiff's costs "to be taxed". In that event the plaintiff's solicitor draws up an "item bill". In that bill the solicitor sets out every step he or she has taken, and the charge he or she wishes to make.

This will cover such items as:

(a) letter before action

(b) drawing form of summons with copy for court
(c) perusing defence
(d) consideration of facts and law
(e) preparing for trial
(f) attending hearing.

It will set out, against each item, the amount the solicitor proposes to charge and will show the time spent on the case.

The bill is lodged with the court and the solicitor then attends the hearing — the "taxation" of his or her bill. The court decides the amount that is fair and reasonable for each item and the total arrived at is the sum payable by the defendant.

That, however, is not the amount the solicitor may charge. It is simply the amount payable by the defendant. Say that for "preparing the trial" the solicitor proposes a charge of £735; the court decides that £250 would be an appropriate sum to be paid *by the defendant*. That means that the solicitor may ask the client to pay the difference — £125.

Again, if the defendant does not pay the taxed costs (or cannot pay them) then the solicitor looks to his or her client to pay the full charges.

It must also be remembered that if a claim is dealt with by arbitration, the plaintiff can only recover the amount as shown on the summons. If the plaintiff instructs a solicitor to attend an arbitration hearing, the plaintiff cannot recover the solicitor's costs for attending that hearing from the defendant.

Defended actions involving solicitors (and sometimes barristers) will thus cost considerable sums of money. When small sums of money are in dispute the costs may well exceed the value of the debt.

For example, in a recent case, the claim was £291 and was defended. The defendant's solicitor requested further and better particulars of the claim. These were prepared and delivered by the plaintiffs' solicitors. The court then gave directions for trial and each side complied. Witness statements were prepared and a date fixed. On the hearing the plaintiffs, in the court's view, proved only £169 and judgment was given in their favour for that sum "with no order as to costs". On a time basis the plaintiffs' solicitors' bill came to £375.

So the question of costs must always be considered. So far as arbitration is concerned creditors should, whenever possible, deal with the matter themselves, without involving solicitors.

When cases are referred to hearing in open court, creditors should monitor costs very carefully. Many solicitors are happy to provide interim bills showing the costs incurred to date, which can assist the monitoring process.

Payments into court

As has been seen the courts do not accept payments from the defendant under a summons. If the defendant wishes to pay the debt, he or she pays the plaintiff.

The court will, however, accept money paid into court "in satisfaction of a claim" in a defended action. Suppose the plaintiff sues for £5000. The defendant delivers a defence, denying liability and then pays £2000 into court. Notice of that payment in is given to the plaintiff. That notice may say that the payment is "in full settlement of the plaintiff's claim" or, it may say, that the payment is "in full settlement of the plaintiff's claim and costs".

Now the plaintiff has a choice: to take the money and, if it was paid "in full settlement of the claim", to seek an order for costs. If it was paid "in full settlement of the claim and costs" he or she can take the money and that is the end of the action.

The plaintiff can, of course, decline to accept the money in court. In that case it stays in court until the action is concluded. However, there is a risk. On the hearing, the judge must not be told of the money that is in court so that his or her decision is on the evidence and the facts, without knowledge of the payment in.

Suppose the judge decides that the plaintiff is entitled to £2000. Now the defendant's solicitor (or counsel) tells the judge that £2000 was paid into court some time ago. The judge will then order that the £2000 be paid out to the plaintiff, but will make no order as to costs. Thus, the plaintiff gets the £2000 but has to pay his or her own legal costs.

This is because the judge has decided that £2000 was the sum due to the plaintiff and the defendant had, in effect, offered that sum before the case came to be determined.

If the judge had decided that more than £2000 was the sum due then, in normal circumstances, the plaintiff would get judgment for the amount the judge felt correct, would get the money in court, and would be entitled to his or her costs.

So long as plaintiffs are awarded more than was paid into court they will get their costs. If they are awarded the amount paid in, or less, they will get that money, but they will have to bear their own legal costs.

As the bulk of the costs will be incurred on the hearing, particularly in cases where counsel are involved, payments into court need to be carefully considered.

Legal aid

The Legal Aid Scheme was devised to ensure that those who need legal advice and representation should not be deprived of it simply because they could not afford the cost of obtaining it. Thus, a person wishing to bring or defend an action may apply for legal aid. He or she goes to a solicitor and completes an application form which sets out the nature of the case and includes any documents to support it. The applicant also gives particulars of income, outgoings, assets and liabilities.

The application goes to a panel of lawyers, who consider the merits of the applicant's case, and to the Department of Social Security which considers the applicant's financial circumstances and assesses how much he or she can afford to pay. The DSS may decide that the applicant can afford nothing, in which case he or she will have a "nil contribution". It may decide that the applicant can afford to pay something and will determine that figure.

If for example, it is decided that the most he or she can afford is £450, he or she will be required to pay that sum by 12 monthly instalments of £37.50 per month.

If the panel of lawyers determine that there is some merit in the applicant's case, a Legal Aid Certificate is issued saying that the applicant is legally aided with a maximum contribution of £450 to be paid at £37.50 per month.

The applicant's chosen solicitor now represents him or her in exactly the same manner as any other client. If counsel needs to be instructed, this will be done. If expert witnesses are required, they will be employed.

The solicitor acting for the legally aided person must give notice to the other side that the client has a Legal Aid Certificate. If the legally aided person is successful in his or her claim, or defence then his or her solicitor's costs are payable by the other side. Those costs go to the Legal Aid Fund, and the solicitor acting for the legally aided person submits a bill to the Legal Aid Authority which pays his or her charges.

If, however, the legally aided person is unsuccessful, then he or she cannot be ordered to pay the costs of the "winner", because this would defeat the aim of the scheme.

If the legally aided person has a "nil contribution" then he or she pays nothing. If he or she has a "maximum contribution" then, so long as he or she pays that sum to the Legal Aid Authority that is the limit of liability.

Although few would question the philosophy that justice should not be denied to those who cannot afford it the scheme does put those facing a legally aided opponent at a financial disadvantage. They have to measure the costs they incur whilst their legally aided opponent does not. Equally, if they win, they will not get their costs. It is also worth noting that if a person qualifies for legal aid it means that it may be difficult for him or her to satisfy any judgment awarded against him or her. His or her income and assets appear to be limited!

Speaking to a group of solicitors on 5 October 1991 the Lord Chancellor expressed the Government's concern at the soaring costs of legal aid. The net cost of the scheme in 1990/91 was £680 million. Costs had been rising by an average of 17 per cent each year. He went on to say:

> One does not have to be a mathematician to recognise that such a high increase each year in the proportion of the national wealth spent on legal aid cannot continue each year . . . [He went on to say that the cost of legal aid was] just about the limit of what is supportable without radical changes.

Changes may come but unless they are very radical, facing an opponent who is legally aided will continue to pose disadvantages concerning costs.

Appendix 1

County Court Directory

ABERDARE

Crown Building
Green Street
Aberdare
Mid. Glam.
CF44 7DW

ABERYSTWYTH

30 Pier Street
Aberystwyth
Dyfed
SY23 2LP

ACCRINGTON

Bradshawgate House
1 Oak Street
Accrington
Lancs
BB5 1EQ

ALDERSHOT and FARNHAM

Copthall House
77/79 Victoria Road
Aldershot
Hants
GU11 1SH

ALFRETON

Crown Building
King Street
Alfreton
Derbys
DE5 7BG

ALNWICK   49 Bondgate Within
                                       Alnwick
                                       Northumberland
                                       NE66 1HZ

ALTRINCHAM   16 Grafton Street
                                       Altrincham
                                       WA14 1DX

AMERSHAM   Law Courts
                                       5 King George V Road
                                       Amersham
                                       Bucks

AMMANFORD   20 College Street
                                       Ammanford
                                       Dyfed
                                       SA19 3AF

ANDOVER   Chantry House
                                       Chantry Way
                                       Andover
                                       Hants
                                       SP10 1NB

ASHFORD   Orchard House
                                       Tannery Lane
                                       Station Road
                                       Ashford
                                       Kent

ASHTON-UNDER-LYNE and   Scotland Street

STALYBRIDGE   Ashton-under-Lyne
                                       Lancs
                                       OL6 6SS

AXMINSTER and CHARD   Chard Street
                                       Axminster
                                       Devon

AYLESBURY   2nd Floor
                                       Heron House
                                       Buckingham Street
                                       Aylesbury
                                       Bucks
                                       HP20 2NQ

BANBURY

35 Parsons Street
Banbury
Oxon
OX16 8BW

BANGOR

Glyn House
High Street
Bangor
Gwynedd

BARGOED

High Street
Bargoed
Mid. Glam.
CF8 8XU

BARNET

Kingmaker House
Station Road
New Barnet
Herts
EN5 1PF

BARNSLEY

12 Regent Street
Barnsley
S. Yorks
S70 2EW

BARNSTAPLE

The Law Courts
Civic Centre
North Walk
Barnstaple
Devon
EX31 1DY

BARROW IN FURNESS and ULVERSTON

Government Buildings
Michaelson Road
Barrow in Furness
Cumbria
LA14 2EZ

BARRY

1st Floor
3/5 Holton Road
Barry
South Glamorgan
CF6 6UE

BASINGSTOKE   4th Floor
                                     Brook House
                                     Churchill Way
                                     Basingstoke
                                     Hants
                                     RG21 1QX

BATH   Trimbridge House
                                     Trim Street
                                     Bath
                                     Avon
                                     BA1 2DJ

BEDFORD   29 Goldington Road
                                     Bedford
                                     MK40 3NN

BERWICK-ON-TWEED   Northam House
                                     15 Walkergate
                                     Berwick-on-Tweed
                                     TD15 1DS

BEVERLEY   74 Lairgate
                                     Beverley
                                     N. Humberside
                                     HU17 8EZ

BIRKENHEAD   76 Hamilton Street
                                     Birkenhead
                                     Merseyside
                                     L41 3EN

BIRMINGHAM   2 Newton Street
                                     Birmingham
                                     B4 7LU

BISHOP AUCKLAND   Station Approach
                                     Newgate Street
                                     Bishop Auckland
                                     Co. Durham
                                     DL14 7HF

BISHOP'S STORTFORD   27 Northgate End
                                     Bishop's Stortford
                                     Herts
                                     CM23 2EZ

BLACKBURN	64 Victoria Street Blackburn Lancs BB1 6DJ
BLACKPOOL	The Law Courts Chapel Street Blackpool Lancs FY1 5RJ
BLACKWOOD	County Court Office Blackwood Road Blackwood Gwent NP2 2XB
BLETCHLEY and LEIGHTON BUZZARD	Block D Bletchley Park Milton Keynes MK3 6LA
BLOOMSBURY and MARYLEBONE	7 Marylebone Road London NW1 5HY
BLYTH	73 Bridge Street Blyth Northumberland NE24 2AL
BODMIN	Cockswell House Market Street Bodmin Cornwall PL31 2JW
BOLTON	The Law Courts Blackhorse Street Bolton BL1 1FV
BOSTON	Crown Buildings Lincoln Lane Boston Lincs PE21 8RV

BOURNEMOUTH   Old Buildings
                                      Law Courts
                                      Stafford Road
                                      Bournemouth
                                      Dorset
                                      BH1 1PN

BOW   96 Romford Road
                                      Stratford
                                      London
                                      E15 4EG

BRADFORD   27–29 Manor Row
                                      Bradford
                                      W. Yorks
                                      BD1 4PT

BRAINTREE   170 Coggeshall Road
                                      Braintree
                                      Essex
                                      CM7 6DQ

BRECON   International Stores Bldgs.
                                      32 High Street
                                      Brecon, Powys
                                      LD3 7AN

BRENTFORD   Alexandra Road
                                      High Street
                                      Brentford, Middx
                                      TW8 0JJ

BRENTWOOD   2a Ingrave Road
                                      Brentwood
                                      Essex
                                      CM15 8BQ

BRIDGEND   Crown Buildings
                                      Angel Street
                                      Bridgend
                                      Mid. Glam.
                                      CF31 4AS

BRIDGNORTH   College House
                                      St. Leonard's Close
                                      Bridgnorth, Salop
                                      WV16 4EN

BRIDGWATER	Court House Queen Street Bridgwater Somerset TA6 3AP
BRIDLINGTON	New Crown Buildings Quay Road Bridlington North Humberside YO16 4LT
BRIGHTON	Law Courts Buildings John Street Brighton, Sussex BN2 2LG
BRISTOL	Greyfriars Lewins Mead Bristol BS1 2NR
BROMLEY	Court House College Road Bromley Kent BR1 3PX
BURNLEY	Bankhouse Street Burnley Lancs BB11 1AJ
BURTON-ON-TRENT	165 Station Street Burton-on-Trent Staffs DE14 1BP
BURY	Tenterden Street Bury Lancs BL9 0H5
BURY ST. EDMUNDS	Triton House St. Andrews Street North Bury St. Edmunds Suffolk IP33 1TR

BUXTON   7/11 Bridge Street
                                          Buxton
                                          Derbys
                                          SK17 6BP

CAERNARVON   Government Buildings
                                          North Penrallt
                                          Caernarvon
                                          Gwynedd
                                          LL55 2XX

CAERPHILLY   Crown Buildings
                                          Florence Grove
                                          Caerphilly
                                          Mid. Glam.
                                          CF8 2WY

CAMBORNE and REDRUTH   Josiah Thomas
                                          Memorial Hall
                                          Fore Street
                                          Camborne
                                          TR14 8AY

CAMBRIDGE   72/80 Hills Road
                                          Cambridge
                                          CB2 1LA

CANTERBURY   Riding Gate House
                                          37 Old Dover Road
                                          Canterbury
                                          Kent
                                          CT1 3JD

CARDIFF   P.O. Box 64
                                          Government Buildings
                                          Westgate Street
                                          Cardiff
                                          S. Glam.
                                          CF1 1NR

CARDIGAN   Government Buildings
                                          Napier Street
                                          Cardigan

CARLISLE   Rufus House
                                          5 Castle Street
                                          Carlisle
                                          Cumbria
                                          CA3 8TG

CARMARTHEN	14 King Street Carmarthen Dyfed
CHATHAM	See Medway
CHELMSFORD	London House New London Road Chelmsford Essex CM2 0QR
CHELTENHAM	The Court House County Court Road Cheltenham Glos GL50 1HB
CHEPSTOW	Station Road Chepstow Gwent NP6 5YD
CHESTER	1 Greyfriars Chester CH1 2NH
CHESTERFIELD	49 Church Way Chesterfield Derbys S40 1SG
CHICHESTER	41/42 Southgate Chichester Sussex PO19 1SX
CHIPPENHAM	23/24 Market Place Chippenham Wilts SN15 3HQ
CHORLEY	Halliwell Street Chorley Lancashire PR7 2AL
CLACTON	See Colchester and Clacton

CLERKENWELL   33 Duncan Terrace
                                     Islington
                                     London
                                     N1 8AN

COLCHESTER and CLACTON   Falkland House
                                     25 Southway
                                     Colchester
                                     Essex
                                     CO3 3EG

CONSETT   Victoria Road
                                     Consett
                                     Co. Durham
                                     DH8 5AU

CONWY   The Old Municipal Offices
                                     Castle Street
                                     Conwy
                                     Gwynedd
                                     LL32 8AY

CORBY   52 Elizabeth Street
                                     Corby
                                     Northants
                                     NN17 1PQ

COVENTRY   22 Warwick Row
                                     Coventry
                                     W. Midlands
                                     CV1 1EY

CREWE   The Law Courts
                                     Civic Centre
                                     Crewe
                                     Cheshire
                                     CW1 2EA

CROYDON   The Law Courts
                                     Barclay Road
                                     Croydon
                                     CR9 1RE

DARLINGTON   4 Coniscliffe Road
                                     Darlington
                                     Co. Durham
                                     DL3 7RG

DARTFORD

Court House
Spital Street
Dartford
Kent
DA1 2EA

DERBY

20 St. Peter's
Church Yard
Derby
DE1 1NP

DEWSBURY

County Court House
Eightlands Road
Dewsbury
W. Yorks
WF13 2PE

DOLGELLAU

Crown Buildings
Arran Road
Dolgellau
Gwynedd

DONCASTER

74 Waterdale
Doncaster
S. Yorks
DN1 3BT

DOVER

72–75 Maison Dieu Road
Dover
Kent
CT17 0TJ

DUDLEY

Priory Road
Dudley
W. Midlands
DY1 3EF

DURHAM

Hallgarth Street
Durham
DH1 3RG

EASTBOURNE

3rd Floor
26 Gildredge Road
Eastbourne
Sussex
BN21 4TA

EAST GRINSTEAD

> East Court
> East Grinstead
> Sussex
> RH19 3LU

EDMONTON

> Court House
> 59 Fore Street
> Upper Edmonton
> London
> N18 2TM

ELLESMERE PORT

> 3 Civic Way
> Ellesmere Port
> Cheshire
> L65 0BB

EPSOM

> The Parade
> Epsom
> Surrey
> KT18 5DN

EVESHAM

> 87 High Street
> Evesham
> Hereford and Worcs
> WR11 4EE

EXETER

> The Castle
> Exeter
> Devon
> EX4 3PS

FOLKESTONE

> Palting House
> Trinity Road
> Folkestone
> Kent
> CT20 2RH

GAINSBOROUGH

> 24 Market Street
> Gainsborough
> Lincs
> DN21 2BH

GATESHEAD

> 1–3 Grahamsley Street
> Gateshead
> Tyne and Wear
> NE8 1LA

GLOUCESTER

First Floor
Barton House
65/71 Barton Street
Gloucester
GL1 1QB

GOOLE

Commerce Chambers
Stanhope Street
Goole
N. Humberside
DN14 5BJ

GRANTHAM

9 Avenue Road
Grantham
Lincs
NG31 6RB

GRAVESEND

25 Pelham Road
Gravesend
Kent
DA11 0HY

GRAYS and THURROCK

Crown House
Crown Road
Grays Thurrock
Essex
RM17 6JB

GREAT GRIMSBY

5th Floor
Crown House
Nelson Street
Grimsby
Humberside
DN32 7SN

GREAT MALVERN

40 Church Street
Great Malvern
WR14 1BR

GREAT YARMOUTH

Haven Bridge House
North Quay
Great Yarmouth
Norfolk

GUILDFORD

The Law Courts
Mary Road
Guildford
Surrey
GU1 4PS

HALIFAX

Prescott Street
Halifax
W. Yorks
HX1 2JJ

HANLEY

53 Regent Road
Hanley
Stoke-on-Trent
Staffs
ST1 3BP

HARLOW

Gate House
The High
Terminus Street
Harlow
CM20 1VW

HARROGATE

12a North Park Road
Harrogate
Yorks
HG1 5PY

HARTLEPOOL

Law Courts
Victoria Road
Hartlepool
Cleveland
TS24 8BS

HASTINGS

The Law Courts
Bohemia Road
Hastings
East Sussex
TN34 1OX

HAVERFORDWEST

Crown Buildings
Cherry Grove
Haverfordwest
Dyfed
SA61 2NN

HAYWARDS HEATH

Concord House
Balcombe Road
Haywards Heath
Sussex
RH16 1NS

HEMEL HEMPSTEAD

1 Seldon Hill
Hemel Hempstead
Herts
HP2 4TX

HEREFORD

First Floor
Barclays Bank Chambers
1/3 Broad Street
Hereford
HR4 9BA

HERTFORD

Sovereign House
Hale Road
Hertford
SG13 8DY

HEXHAM

Hadrian House
21 Market Street
Hexham
Northumberland
NE46 3NQ

HIGH WYCOMBE

The Law Courts
Easton Street
High Wycombe
HP11 1LR

HINCKLEY

8a Rugby Road
Hinckley
Leics
LE10 0QF

HITCHIN

2nd Floor
Station House
Nightingale Road
Hitchin
Herts
SG5 1LX

HOLYWELL

County Court Buildings
Holywell
Clwyd
CH8 7TE

HORSHAM

The Law Courts
Hurst Road
Horsham
Sussex
RH12 2ET

HUDDERSFIELD	County Court House Queen Street Huddersfield W. Yorks HD1 2SL
HULL	See Kingston-upon-Hull
HUNTINGDON	Government Offices Chequers Court Huntingdon Cambs PE18 6LX
HYDE	2nd Floor 1c Market Place Hyde Cheshire SK14 2QF
ILFORD	Buckingham Road Ilford Essex IG1 1TP
ILKESTON	31a Albert Street Ilkeston Derbyshire DE7 8GU
IPSWICH	8 Arcade Street Ipswich Suffolk IP1 1EJ
KEIGHLEY	Yorkshire Bank Chambers North Street Keighley West Yorks BD21 3SH
KENDAL	12/14 Stricklandgate Kendal Cumbria
KETTERING	3 Bowling Green Road Kettering Northants NN15 7DY

KIDDERMINSTER   Comberton Place
                                       Kidderminster
                                       Hereford and Worcs
                                       DY10 1QR

KING'S LYNN   London Road
                                       King's Lynn
                                       Norfolk
                                       PE30 5PU

KINGSTON-UPON-HULL   Commerce House
                                       Paragon Street
                                       Kingston-upon-Hull
                                       Humberside
                                       HU1 3PS

KINGSTON UPON THAMES   St. James Road
                                       Kingston upon Thames
                                       KT1 2AD

LAMBETH   Court House
                                       Cleaver Street
                                       Kennington Road
                                       London
                                       SE11 4DZ

LAMPETER   Crown Buildings
                                       Pontfaen Road
                                       Lampeter
                                       Dyfed

LANCASTER   18a Arndale House
                                       Common Garden Street
                                       Lancaster
                                       Lancs
                                       LA1 1UY

LAUNCESTON   32 Broad Street
                                       Launceston
                                       Cornwall

LEEDS   1 Oxford Row
                                       Leeds
                                       LS1 3BE

LEICESTER   Lower Hill Street
                                       Leicester
                                       LE1 3SJ

LEIGH

22 Walmesley Road
Leigh
WN7 1YF

LEOMINSTER

91 Etnam Street
Leominster
Hereford and Worcs
HR6 8AF

LEWES

The Law Courts
High Street
Lewes
Sussex
BN7 1YB

LICHFIELD

Wade Street
Lichfield
Staffs
WS13 6HL

LINCOLN

Mill House
Brayford Side North
Lincoln
LN1 1YW

LIVERPOOL

New Law Courts
Derby Square
Liverpool
L2 1XA

LLANDRINDOD WELLS

"Deauville"
Spa Road
Llandrindod Wells
Powys
LD1 5AB

LLANELLI

Court Buildings
Town Hall Square
Llanelli
Dyfed
SA15 3AH

LLANGEFNI

2nd Floor
4 Church Street
Llangefni
Gwynedd

LOUGHBOROUGH	Crown House Southfield Road Loughborough Leics LE11 2YS
LOWESTOFT	"Lyndhurst" 28 Gordon Road Lowestoft Suffolk NR32 1NL
LUDLOW	9–10 King Street Ludlow Salop SY8 1QW
LUTON	2nd Floor Cresta House Alma Street Luton Beds LU1 2PU
MACCLESFIELD	4th Floor London and Manchester House 32 Park Green Macclesfield SK11 7QP
MAIDSTONE	The Law Courts Barker Road Maidstone ME16 8EQ
MALDON	London Road Maldon Essex CM9 6NE
MALTON	c/o York County Court 4 New Street York YO1 2SB
MANCHESTER	19a Quay Street Manchester M60 9DJ

MANSFIELD   Clerkson House
                                            St. Peters Way
                                            Mansfield
                                            Notts
                                            NG18 1BQ

MARGATE   See Thanet

MARKET DRAYTON   Cheshire Street
                                            Market Drayton
                                            Salop
                                            TF9 1RN

MATLOCK   Imperial Chambers
                                            73 Dale Road
                                            Matlock
                                            Derbys
                                            DE4 3LT

MAYOR'S and CITY OF LONDON   Guildhall
                                            Basinghall Street
                                            London
                                            EC2V 5AQ

MEDWAY   Anchorage House
                                            High Street
                                            Chatham
                                            Kent
                                            ME4 4DW

MELTON MOWBRAY   50/52 Scalford Road
                                            Melton Mowbray
                                            Leics
                                            LE13 1JY

MERTHYR TYDFIL   The Law Courts
                                            Glebeland Place
                                            Merthyr Tydfil
                                            Mid. Glam.
                                            CF47 8BU

MIDDLESBROUGH   Wilson Street West
                                            Middlesbrough
                                            Cleveland
                                            TS1 1SG

MILTON KEYNES   See Bletchley

MOLD

Law Courts
County Civic Centre
Mold
Clwyd
CH7 1AE

MONMOUTH

Market Hall
Priory Street
Monmouth
Gwent
NP5 3XA

MORPETH

17 Market Place
Morpeth
Northumberland
NE16 1LZ

NEATH and PORT TALBOT

The Parade
Neath
West Glam.
SA11 1AL

NELSON

Phoenix Chambers
9/13 Holme Street
Nelson
Lancs
BB9 0SS

NEWARK

The County Court
Crown Building
41 Lombard Street
Newark
Notts
NG24 1XN

NEWBURY

Kings Road West
Newbury
Berks
RG14 5AH

NEWCASTLE UPON TYNE

56 Westgate Road
Newcastle upon Tyne
NE1 5UR

NEWPORT (I.O.W.)

130/132 High Street
Newport I.O.W.
PO30 1TP

NEWPORT (Gwent)	Olympia House
	3rd Floor
	Upper Dock Street
	Newport
	Gwent
	NPT 1PQ

NEWTON ABBOT	Bridge House
	Courtenay Street
	Newton Abbot
	Devon
	TQ12 2QT

NEWTOWN	Ladywell House
	Newtown
	Powys
	SY16 1AF

NORTHALLERTON	Government Buildings
	Crosby Road
	Northallerton
	N. Yorks
	DL6 1AD

NORTHAMPTON	St Katherine's House
	50 Gold Street
	Northampton
	NN1 1RS

NORTH SHIELDS	Northumbria House
	Norfolk Street
	North Shields
	NE30 1EX

NORTHWICH	25/27 High Street
	Northwich
	Cheshire
	CW9 5DB

NORWICH	Norvic House
	29/33 Chapelfield Road
	Norwich
	NR2 1SS

NOTTINGHAM	St. Peter's Gate
	Nottingham
	NG1 7EJ

NUNEATON	Heron House Newdegate Street Nuneaton Warwickshire CV11 4EL
OLDHAM	Church Lane Oldham OL1 3AR
OSWESTRY	35 Church Street Oswestry Salop SY11 2SZ
OTLEY	Bondgate House 11 Bondgate Otley W. Yorks LS21 3AB
OXFORD	Harcourt House Marston Road Oxford OX3 0EF
PENRITH	The Court House Lowther Terrace Penrith CA11 7QL
PENZANCE	Trevear Alverton Penzance Cornwall TR18 2QY
PETERBOROUGH	1 Laxton Square Peterborough PE1 1TR
PLYMOUTH	The Law Courts Armada Way Plymouth Devon PL1 2ER

PONTEFRACT

Horsefair House
Horsefair
Pontefract
W. Yorks
WF8 1RJ

PONTYPOOL

P.O. Box 12
Royal House
George Street
Pontypool
Gwent
NP4 6XH

PONTYPRIDD

Courthouse Street
Pontypridd
M. Glamorgan
CF37 1JR

POOLE

Law Courts
Civic Centre
Park Road
Poole
BH15 2NS

PORTHMADOG

Thedford House
High Street
Porthmadog
Gwynedd
LL49 9LS

PORTSMOUTH

County Court Buildings
Winston Churchill Avenue
Portsmouth
Hants
PO1 2DL

PRESTON

Robert House
2 Starkie Street
Preston
Lancs
PR1 3HB

RAWTENSTALL

1 Grange Street
Rawtenstall
Rossendale
Lancs
BB4 7RT

READING

First Floor
10 Friars Walk
Friar Street
Reading
Berks
RG1 1LA

REDDITCH

43 Unicorn Hill
Redditch
Hereford and Worcs
B97 4QT

REIGATE

Law Courts
Hatchlands Road
Redhill
Surrey
RH1 6BL

RHYL

64 Brighton Road
Rhyl
Clwyd
LL18 3HR

ROCHDALE

Fleece Street
Rochdale
OL16 1ND

ROMFORD

2a Oaklands Avenue
Romford
Essex
RM1 4DP

ROTHERHAM

Portland House
Mansfield Road
Rotherham
S. Yorks
S60 2BX

RUGBY

5 Newbold Road
Rugby
W. Midlands
CV21 2RN

RUNCORN

The Law Courts
Shopping City
Runcorn
Cheshire
WA7 2HA

ST. ALBANS   36/38 London Road
                                    St. Albans
                                    Herts
                                    AL1 1NG

ST. AUSTELL   Duchy House
                                    Lower Aylmer Square
                                    (Trinity Street Entrance)
                                    St. Austell
                                    Cornwall
                                    PL25 5LQ

ST. HELENS   1st Floor
                                    Rexmore House
                                    Cotham Street
                                    St. Helens
                                    Merseyside
                                    WA10 1SE

SALFORD   Encombe Place
                                    Salford
                                    M60 9HA

SALISBURY   Cheviot House
                                    Castle Street
                                    Salisbury
                                    Wilts
                                    SP1 3TL

SCARBOROUGH   9 Northway
                                    Scarborough
                                    N. Yorks
                                    YO11 2EH

SCUNTHORPE   Crown Building
                                    Comforts Avenue
                                    Scunthorpe
                                    S. Humberside
                                    DN15 6PR

SEVENOAKS   Boswell's House
                                    44 London Road
                                    Sevenoaks
                                    Kent

SHAFTESBURY   c/o Yeovil County Court
                                    20 Kingston
                                    Yeovil
                                    BA20 2QD

SHEERNESS

Magistrates' Courts
Bridge Road
Sheerness
Kent

SHEFFIELD

Belgrave House
Bank Street
Sheffield
S. Yorks
S1 1EH

SHOREDITCH

19 Leonard Street
London
EC2A 4AL

SHREWSBURY

2nd Floor
Mardol House
Market Hall Buildings
Shoplatch
Shrewsbury
SY1 1HS

SITTINGBOURNE

Revenue House
Central Avenue
Sittingbourne
Kent
ME10 4BU

SKEGNESS and SPILSBY

Town Hall Annexe
North Parade
Skegness

SKIPTON

Otley Street
Skipton
N. Yorks
BD23 1EH

SLEAFORD

Spur E
Eastgate
Sleaford
Lincs
NG34 7SJ

SLOUGH

The Law Courts
Windsor Road
Slough
Berks
SL1 2HE

SOUTHAMPTON   Ulster House
                                             Lower Canal Walk
                                             Southampton
                                             Hants
                                             SO9 5AF

SOUTHEND   The Court House
                                             Victoria Avenue
                                             Southend-on-Sea
                                             Essex
                                             SS2 6ET

SOUTHPORT   34 Hoghton Street
                                             Southport
                                             Merseyside
                                             PR9 0PU

SOUTH SHIELDS   25–26 Market Place
                                             South Shields
                                             Tyne and Wear
                                             NE33 1AG

SPALDING   Post Office Building
                                             5a Sheep Market
                                             Spalding
                                             Lincolnshire
                                             PE11 4AQ

STAFFORD   15 Crabbery Street
                                             Stafford
                                             ST16 2BA

STAINES   The Law Courts
                                             Knowle Green
                                             Staines
                                             Middlesex
                                             TW18 1XH

STAMFORD   12 Broad Street
                                             Stamford
                                             Lincs
                                             PE9 1PG

STOCKPORT   "Heron House"
                                             Wellington Street
                                             Stockport
                                             SK1 3DJ

STOCKTON-ON-TEES

4 Bridge Road
Stockton-on-Tees
Cleveland
TS18 3BS

STOKE-ON-TRENT

53 Regent Road
Hanley
Stoke-on-Trent
Staffs
ST1 3BP

STOURBRIDGE

Hagley Road
Stourbridge
W. Midlands
DY18 1QL

STRATFORD-ON-AVON

Russell House
Ely Street
Stratford-on-Avon
Warwickshire
CV37 6LF

STROUD

George Street
Stroud
Gloucestershire
GL5 3DR

SUDBURY

1st Floor
Borehamgate House
Borehamgate Precinct
King Street
Sudbury
Suffolk
CO10 6ED

SUNDERLAND

John Street
Sunderland
Tyne and Wear
SR1 1RB

SWANSEA

Government Buildings
St. Mary's Square
Swansea
West Glam.
SA1 3LL

SWINDON	County Court Buildings Clarence Street Swindon Wilts SN1 2JE
TAMWORTH	12 The Precinct Lower Gungate Tamworth Staffs B79 7AJ
TAUNTON	35/36 High Street Taunton Somerset TA1 3ST
THANET	Capital House Northdown Road Margate Kent CT9 1EQ
THORNE	Orchard Street Thorne S. Yorks DN8 5EH
TODMORDEN	The Weavers Institute Burnley Road Todmorden W. Yorks OL14 5LH
TONBRIDGE	Crown Buildings Bradford Street Tonbridge Kent
TORQUAY	Castle Chambers Union Street Torquay Devon TQ1 4BS
TROWBRIDGE	5 Fore Street Trowbridge Wilts BA14 8ND

TRURO

"Trevint"
Strangways Villas
Truro
Cornwall
TR1 2PB

TUNBRIDGE WELLS

Merevale House
42/46 London Road
Tunbridge Wells
Kent
TN1 1DN

UXBRIDGE

114 High Street
Uxbridge
Middx
UB8 1DF

WAKEFIELD

Crown House
127 Kirkgate
Wakefield
W. Yorks
WF1 1JW

WALSALL

Lichfield Street
Walsall
W. Midlands
WS1 1TL

WANDSWORTH

76 Upper Richmond Road
Putney
London
SW15 2SU

WARRINGTON

Palmyra Square South
Warrington
Cheshire
WA1 1JR

WARWICK

Northgate
South Side
Warwick
CV34 4RB

WATFORD

Cassiobury House
11/19 Station Road
Watford
Herts

WELLINGBOROUGH

Lothersdale House
West Villa Road
Wellingborough
Northants
NN8 4NF

WELLINGTON (Salop)

Crown Buildings
Walker Street
Wellington
Telford
Salop
TF1 1DY

WELSHPOOL

The Mansion House
Severn Street
Welshpool
Powys
SY21 7AD

WEST BROMWICH

2nd Floor
Spencer House
335/337 High Street
West Bromwich
W. Midlands
B70 8RF

WEST LONDON

43 North End Road
W. Kensington
London
W14 8SZ

WESTMINSTER

82 St. Martin's Lane
London
WC2N 4AG

WESTON-SUPER-MARE

Lloyds Bank Chambers
115 High Street
Weston-super-Mare
Avon
BS23 1HH

WEYMOUTH

2nd Floor
Westwey House
Westwey Road
Weymouth
Dorset
DT4 8TE

WHITBY

Golden Lion Bank
Whitby
N. Yorks
YO12 3BS

WHITEHAVEN

13 Sandhills Lane
Whitehaven
Cumbria
CA28 7NJ

WIGAN

Crawford Street
Wigan
WN1 1NG

WILLESDEN

9 Action Lane
Harlesden
London
NW10 8UX

WINCHESTER

South Side Offices
The Law Courts
The Castle
Winchester
Hants
SO23 9DL

WISBECH

Albion House
Albion Place
Wisbech
Cambs
PE13 1AG

WOLVERHAMPTON

50 Queen Street
Wolverhampton
W. Midlands
WV1 3BS

WOOLWICH

The Court House
Powis Street
London
SE18 6JW

WORCESTER

44 Foregate Street
Worcester
WR1 1EQ

WORKINGTON	Langdale House Gray Street Workington Cumbria CA14 2PA
WORKSOP	8 Slack Walk Worksop Notts S80 1LN
WORTHING	The Law Courts Christchurch Road Worthing Sussex BN11 1JD
WREXHAM	2nd Floor 31 Chester Street Wrexham Clwyd
YEOVIL	20 Kingston Yeovil Somerset BA20 2QD
YORK	4 New Street York YO1 2SB

Appendix 2

Court Fees

For the issue of a default summons:	Claims up to £300	10p in the £1 or part £1 with a minimum fee of £7
	Claims over £300 up to £500	£37
	Claims over £500	£43
On request for service by bailiff:		£5
On issue of a warrant of execution:		15p in the £1 with a minimum fee of £5 and a maximum of £38
Attachment of earnings:		10p in every £1 with a minimum fee of £5 and a maximum of £40
On issuing garnishee proceedings:		£12
On application for a charging order:		£12
Fee on writ of fi.fa. — High Court:		£10

Appendix 3

Flow Chart of Court Action

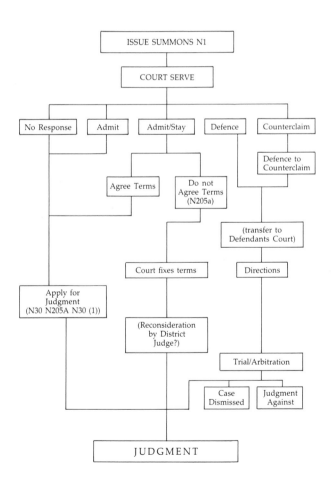

Index